REALSIMPLE

dinner tonight: done!

quick & delicious recipes

spring/summer 2011

recipes edited by
Allie Lewis Clapp and Lygeia Grace

REALSIMPLE

It's 5 P.M.—do you know where tonight's dinner is? Why is that such a hard question to answer? Because, in no particular order: You're busy; you have a family; you have a job; you have a hobby; you're reading a great book; you're watching pets do funny things on YouTube; you're cleaning the bathroom; you're catching up with an old friend; you're planning your next vacation; you (gasp!) hate to cook. Or you simply have better things to do than spend all afternoon planning and preparing a meal that will take all of 15 minutes to consume.

Besides, Allie Lewis Clapp has the answer for you. As *Real Simple*'s food director, she, along with her talented team, is the genius responsible for the 81 recipes in this book and therefore for your happiness tonight and tomorrow night and for many nights to come. Whether you want to build your dinner around meat or vegetables, in just half an hour or in only one pot, here you'll find delicious, healthy, easy dinners that will allow you to watch YouTube, read a book, or work really hard all afternoon and still have a satisfying meal in front of you by sundown. And, if you're up to it, a nice little dessert to finish.

But wait, you say, what if the cupboard is bare? No worries: We've got you covered. You may not be able to make our Thai Red Curry Chicken (not everyone has red curry paste in her pantry), but chances are you've got ground beef, canned tomatoes and some kind of noodles—in which case you could make Pappardelle with Spicy Meat Sauce without a trip to the market. The recipes use only real, whole ingredients, span cultures (from Moroccan Chicken Salad to Sweet and Spicy Beef Stir-fry), and are accompanied by helpful tips, tricks, and substitutions. You'll also find the nutritional breakdown for every recipe (page 154).

It's 5 P.M.—do you know where tonight's dinner is? Of course you do. It's right here. Find it, make it, and enjoy.

Kristin van Ogtrop
Managing Editor, *Real Simple*

dinner tonight:
appetizers

prosciutto-fennel crostini

hands-on time: 15 minutes / total time: 15 minutes
serves 8

24 thin slices baguette
 3 tablespoons olive oil
 1 small fennel bulb—quartered, cored, and
   thinly sliced
 2 tablespoons chopped fresh flat-leaf parsley
 1 tablespoon fresh lemon juice
   Kosher salt and black pepper
½ pound thinly sliced prosciutto

▶ Heat oven to 375° F. Place the baguette slices
on a baking sheet and brush both sides with
2 tablespoons of the oil. Toast until golden, 10 to
12 minutes.

▶ Meanwhile, in a small bowl, toss the fennel
and parsley with the lemon juice, the remaining
tablespoon of oil, ¼ teaspoon salt, and ⅛ teaspoon pepper.

▶ Dividing evenly, top the baguette slices with
the prosciutto and fennel mixture.

radishes with creamy ricotta

hands-on time: 5 minutes / total time: 5 minutes
serves 4

 1 cup ricotta (preferably fresh)
 1 tablespoon olive oil
   Kosher salt and black pepper
16 radishes, halved if large

▶ Place the ricotta in a small bowl, drizzle with
the oil, and season with ⅛ teaspoon each salt
and pepper. Serve with the radishes.

smoked salmon pizzettes

hands-on time: 5 minutes / total time: 30 minutes
serves 4

- 1 pound pizza dough, thawed if frozen
  Cornmeal, for the pan
- 2 shallots, sliced
- $\frac{1}{2}$ cup crème fraîche or sour cream
- 4 ounces sliced smoked salmon
- 2 tablespoons capers
- 2 tablespoons chopped fresh chives

▶ Heat oven to 425° F. Shape the dough into 4 small rounds and place on a cornmeal-dusted rimmed baking sheet.

▶ Sprinkle the dough with the shallots, pressing them in gently, and spread with the crème fraîche. Bake until golden brown, 20 to 25 minutes.

▶ Top the pizzettes with the smoked salmon and sprinkle with the capers and chives.

grilled teriyaki wings

hands-on time: 15 minutes / total time: 30 minutes
serves 4

- 8 chicken wings (about $1\frac{1}{2}$ pounds total)
- $\frac{1}{4}$ cup teriyaki sauce, plus more for serving
- $\frac{1}{2}$ teaspoon toasted sesame seeds

▶ Heat grill to medium-low. Halve each wing through the joint; cut off and discard the wing tip.

▶ Grill the wings, covered, turning occasionally, until cooked through, 20 to 25 minutes. During the last 5 minutes of grilling, brush with the teriyaki sauce.

▶ Sprinkle the wings with the sesame seeds and serve with the additional teriyaki sauce for dipping.

artichoke and spinach relish with walnuts

hands-on time: 10 minutes / total time: 15 minutes
serves 8 (makes 1½ cups)

¼ cup walnuts
1 13.75-ounce can artichoke hearts, rinsed
  and chopped
1 cup baby spinach, chopped
¼ cup grated Parmesan (1 ounce)
3 tablespoons mayonnaise
2 tablespoons fresh lemon juice
  Kosher salt and black pepper
  Crackers and cut-up vegetables, for serving

▶ Heat oven to 400° F. Spread the walnuts on a rimmed baking sheet and toast, tossing occasionally, until fragrant, 6 to 8 minutes. Let cool, then roughly chop.

▶ In a small bowl, combine the artichoke hearts, spinach, Parmesan, mayonnaise, lemon juice, walnuts, ¼ teaspoon salt, and ⅛ teaspoon pepper. Serve with the crackers and vegetables.

creamy salmon spread with horseradish

hands-on time: 10 minutes / total time: 10 minutes
serves 8 (makes 1½ cups)

8 ounces cream cheese, at room temperature
2 tablespoons prepared horseradish
2 tablespoons chopped fresh dill
  Kosher salt and black pepper
4 ounces smoked salmon, chopped
  Crackers and cut-up vegetables, for serving

▶ In a small bowl, combine the cream cheese, horseradish, dill, ½ teaspoon salt, and ⅛ teaspoon pepper.

▶ Fold the salmon into the cream cheese mixture. Serve with the crackers and vegetables.

double tomato crostini

**hands-on time: 10 minutes / total time: 15 minutes
serves 4**

12 slices baguette
 1 tablespoon olive oil
¼ cup sun-dried tomato spread
 1 cup cherry tomatoes, cut up
    Kosher salt and black pepper

▸ Heat oven to 375° F. Place the baguette slices
on a baking sheet and brush both sides with the
oil. Toast until golden, 10 to 12 minutes.

▸ Dividing evenly, top the toasted baguette slices
with the tomato spread and tomatoes. Season
with ¼ teaspoon each salt and pepper.

five-minute hummus

**hands-on time: 5 minutes / total time: 5 minutes
serves 6 (makes 1½ cups)**

 1 15.5-ounce can chickpeas, rinsed
 1 clove garlic
¼ cup plus 1 tablespoon olive oil
 2 tablespoons fresh lemon juice
 2 tablespoons tahini (sesame seed paste; optional)
 1 teaspoon ground cumin
    Kosher salt
¼ teaspoon paprika
    Pitas, for serving (optional)

▸ In a food processor, puree the chickpeas, garlic,
¼ cup of the oil, lemon juice, tahini (if desired),
cumin, and ¾ teaspoon salt until smooth and
creamy. Add 1 to 2 tablespoons water as necessary to achieve the desired consistency.

▸ Transfer the chickpea mixture to a small bowl.
Drizzle with the remaining tablespoon of oil
and sprinkle with the paprika just before serving.
Serve with the pitas, if desired.

shrimp skewers with Feta-dill sauce

hands-on time: 15 minutes / total time: 20 minutes
serves 4

2 ounces Feta, crumbled ($^1/_2$ cup)
1 tablespoon chopped fresh dill
5 tablespoons olive oil
  Kosher salt and black pepper
1 pound peeled and deveined large shrimp

▶ Soak 8 wooden skewers in water for 10 minutes. Heat grill to medium-high.

▶ In a small bowl, combine the Feta, dill, 4 tablespoons of the oil, and ⅛ teaspoon pepper.

▶ Thread the shrimp onto the skewers. Brush with the remaining tablespoon of oil and season with ¼ teaspoon each salt and pepper. Grill until opaque throughout, 2 to 3 minutes per side. Drizzle with the Feta sauce before serving.

sweet pea and ricotta crostini

hands-on time: 10 minutes / total time: 20 minutes
serves 4

16 thin slices baguette
 4 tablespoons olive oil
 1 10-ounce package frozen peas, thawed
$^1/_2$ cup ricotta
 1 scallion, coarsely chopped
 1 ounce Parmesan, cut into pieces, plus more, grated, for topping
   Kosher salt and black pepper

▶ Heat oven to 375° F. Place the baguette slices on a baking sheet and brush both sides with 2 tablespoons of the oil. Toast until golden, 10 to 12 minutes.

▶ Meanwhile, in a food processor, puree the peas, ricotta, scallion, and Parmesan with the remaining 2 tablespoons of oil, ½ teaspoon salt, and ¼ teaspoon pepper, scraping down the sides of the bowl occasionally, until the Parmesan has broken down and the mixture is nearly smooth.

▶ Spread the pea mixture on the toasts and sprinkle with the grated Parmesan.

dinner tonight:
salads

creamy shrimp salad with endive and cucumber

hands-on time: 10 minutes / total time: 10 minutes / serves 4

¼ cup buttermilk
¼ cup sour cream
½ cup cornichons, sliced, plus
   3 tablespoons of the brine
   Kosher salt and black pepper
1 head Boston lettuce, torn
   (about 6 cups)
2 heads endive, sliced
1 pound cooked peeled and
   deveined medium shrimp
1 small English cucumber,
   halved lengthwise and
   thinly sliced crosswise
6 small radishes, thinly sliced
2 tablespoons chopped fresh
   tarragon

▶ In a small bowl, whisk together the buttermilk, sour cream, cornichon brine, and ¼ teaspoon each salt and pepper.

▶ In a large bowl, combine the lettuce, endive, shrimp, cucumber, radishes, tarragon, and cornichons and toss with the dressing.

TIP
Tarragon, an herb commonly used in French cooking, tastes like a combination of basil and licorice. Either parsley or basil is a fine substitute in this recipe.

turkey Waldorf salad

hands-on time: 5 minutes / total time: 10 minutes / serves 4

- 2 tablespoons sour cream
- 2 tablespoons mayonnaise
- 1 tablespoon white wine vinegar
  Kosher salt and black pepper
- 1 cup shredded roasted turkey or chicken
- 1 celery stalk, sliced
- 1 Granny Smith apple, cut into $\frac{1}{2}$-inch pieces
- 2 tablespoons chopped toasted walnuts
- 1 small head red leaf lettuce, torn

▶ In a medium bowl, whisk together the sour cream, mayonnaise, vinegar, ½ teaspoon salt, and ¼ teaspoon pepper. Add the turkey, celery, apple, and walnuts and toss to combine.

▶ Divide the lettuce among bowls and top with the turkey mixture.

TIP
To toast walnuts, spread them on a rimmed baking sheet and cook in a 350° F oven, tossing occasionally, until fragrant, 8 to 10 minutes.

minty bulgur salad with salmon and cucumbers

hands-on time: 30 minutes / total time: 30 minutes / serves 4

1 tablespoon plus 1 teaspoon olive oil

1 pound skinless salmon fillet
Kosher salt and black pepper

1 cup bulgur

2 Kirby cucumbers, halved lengthwise and thinly sliced crosswise

1 cup fresh flat-leaf parsley leaves

¼ cup torn fresh mint leaves

½ small red onion, thinly sliced

3 tablespoons fresh lemon juice

▶ Heat 1 teaspoon of the oil in a large nonstick skillet over medium heat. Season the salmon with ¼ teaspoon each salt and pepper and cook until opaque throughout, 4 to 6 minutes per side. Transfer to a plate and refrigerate until cool, about 15 minutes. Using a fork, flake the salmon into large pieces.

▶ Meanwhile, in a large bowl, combine the bulgur with 2 cups boiling water. Let stand until tender, about 25 minutes.

▶ Drain the bulgur and return it to the bowl. Add the cucumbers, parsley, mint, and onion and toss with the lemon juice, the remaining tablespoon of oil, ½ teaspoon salt, and ¼ teaspoon pepper. Gently fold in the salmon.

TIP
Made from steamed, dried, and cracked wheat, bulgur has a nutty flavor and a grainy texture that make it great for salads (think tabbouleh). If you like, substitute wild or brown rice, barley, or couscous, cooked according to the package directions.

romaine salad with tomatoes and bacon

hands-on time: 15 minutes / total time: 15 minutes
serves 4

- 4 slices bacon
- 1/4 cup olive oil
- 1/4 cup grated Parmesan (1 ounce)
- 2 tablespoons sour cream
- 1 tablespoon white wine vinegar
  Kosher salt and black pepper
- 1 head romaine lettuce, cut into strips (about 6 cups)
- 1 cup grape tomatoes, halved
- 4 scallions, sliced

▶ In a skillet, cook the bacon over medium heat until crisp, 6 to 8 minutes. Transfer to a paper towel–lined plate. Break into pieces when cool.

▶ In a small bowl, whisk together the oil, Parmesan, sour cream, vinegar, 2 tablespoons water, and 1/8 teaspoon each salt and pepper.

▶ In a large bowl, combine the lettuce, tomatoes, scallions, and bacon and toss with the dressing.

mesclun salad with chickpeas and dried cherries

hands-on time: 10 minutes / total time: 10 minutes
serves 4

- 3 tablespoons olive oil
- 2 tablespoons balsamic vinegar
- 1 teaspoon Dijon mustard
  Kosher salt and black pepper
- 6 ounces mesclun (about 6 cups)
- 2 carrots, halved lengthwise and thinly sliced on the bias
- 1 15.5-ounce can chickpeas, rinsed
- 1/2 cup dried cherries
- 1/4 cup fresh dill sprigs

▶ In a small bowl, whisk together the oil, vinegar, mustard, 1/4 teaspoon salt, and 1/8 teaspoon pepper.

▶ In a large bowl, combine the mesclun, carrots, chickpeas, cherries, and dill and toss with the dressing.

arugula salad with green beans and radishes

hands-on time: 10 minutes / total time: 10 minutes
serves 4

- ¼ cup olive oil
- ¼ cup grated Parmesan (1 ounce)
- 2 tablespoons sour cream
- 1 tablespoon white wine vinegar
  Kosher salt and black pepper
- 1 large bunch arugula (about 6 cups)
- 1 small fennel bulb, cored and very thinly sliced
- ¼ pound raw green beans, cut into 1-inch pieces (about 1¼ cups)
- 6 radishes, cut into wedges

▶ In a small bowl, whisk together the oil, Parmesan, sour cream, vinegar, 2 tablespoons water, and ⅛ teaspoon each salt and pepper.

▶ In a large bowl, combine the arugula, fennel, green beans, and radishes and toss with the dressing.

watercress salad with beets and Feta

hands-on time: 10 minutes / total time: 10 minutes
serves 4

- 2 tablespoons olive oil
- 2 tablespoons fresh lemon juice
- 1 teaspoon honey
- ½ shallot, finely chopped
  Kosher salt and black pepper
- 2 bunches watercress, thick stems removed (about 6 cups)
- 1 15-ounce can whole beets, drained and thinly sliced
- 2 ounces Feta, crumbled (½ cup)

▶ In a small bowl, whisk together the oil, lemon juice, honey, shallot, ¼ teaspoon salt, and ⅛ teaspoon pepper.

▶ In a large bowl, combine the watercress and beets and toss with the dressing. Sprinkle with the Feta.

chopped steak salad

hands-on time: 15 minutes / total time: 15 minutes / serves 4

¾ pound flank steak
   Kosher salt and black pepper
1 head romaine lettuce,
   chopped
2 cups chopped red cabbage
1 15.5-ounce can cannellini
   beans, rinsed
½ cup chopped roasted
   red peppers
¼ cup chopped fresh flat-
   leaf parsley
¼ cup store-bought vinaigrette

▶ Heat broiler. Season the steak with ½ teaspoon salt and ¼ teaspoon black pepper and place on a broiler-proof rimmed baking sheet.

▶ Broil the steak to the desired doneness, 4 to 5 minutes per side for medium-rare. Let rest for 5 minutes, then cut into small pieces.

▶ Meanwhile, in a large bowl, combine the lettuce, cabbage, beans, roasted red peppers, parsley, and steak and toss with the vinaigrette.

TIP
This salad is a tasty way to use up leftover steak (or lamb or pork) from last night's dinner.

Moroccan chicken salad with carrots

hands-on time: 20 minutes / total time: 20 minutes / serves 4

5 tablespoons olive oil
8 small chicken cutlets (about
   1½ pounds total)
1 teaspoon ground cumin
   Kosher salt and black pepper
3 tablespoons fresh lime juice
¼ teaspoon crushed red pepper
5 ounces baby spinach
   (about 6 cups)
2 cups fresh cilantro leaves
4 carrots, peeled into strips
   with a vegetable peeler
½ cup raisins

▸ Heat 2 tablespoons of the oil in a large skillet over medium-high heat. Season the chicken with the cumin, ½ teaspoon salt, and ¼ teaspoon black pepper. In batches, cook the chicken until golden brown and cooked through, about 2 minutes per side. Cut into strips.

▸ In a small bowl, whisk together the lime juice, red pepper, the remaining 3 tablespoons of oil, and ½ teaspoon salt.

▸ In a large bowl, combine the spinach, chicken, cilantro, carrots, and raisins and toss with the dressing.

TIP
To make this easy recipe even faster, substitute shredded rotisserie chicken for the cooked cutlets.

grilled salmon salad with grapefruit

hands-on time: 20 minutes / total time: 20 minutes / serves 4

4 6-ounce pieces skinless
   salmon fillet
   Kosher salt and black pepper
1 grapefruit
4 cups mixed greens
1 avocado, diced
¼ small red onion, sliced
2 tablespoons olive oil
2 teaspoons red wine vinegar

▸ Heat grill to medium. Season the salmon with ½ teaspoon salt and ¼ teaspoon pepper and grill until opaque throughout, 5 to 6 minutes per side. Transfer to a plate and refrigerate for 5 minutes. Using a fork, flake the salmon into large pieces.

▸ Meanwhile, cut away the peel and pith of the grapefruit. Working over a large bowl, cut along the membranes between segments to release them, adding them to the bowl as you go.

▸ Add the greens, avocado, and onion to the bowl and gently toss with the oil, vinegar, and ¼ teaspoon each salt and pepper. Serve the salad topped with the salmon.

TIP
Instead of grilling the salmon, you can cook it in 1 table-spoon of oil in a large skillet over medium heat until opaque throughout, 5 to 6 minutes per side.

dinner tonight:
poultry

braised chicken and spring vegetables

hands-on time: 15 minutes / total time: 40 minutes / serves 4

1 tablespoon olive oil
8 small bone-in chicken thighs
   (about 2¹/₂ pounds total)
   Kosher salt and black pepper
1 cup low-sodium chicken broth
12 medium radishes, halved
³/₄ pound carrots (about 4),
   cut into sticks
1 teaspoon sugar
2 tablespoons chopped fresh
   chives

▶ Heat the oil in a Dutch oven over medium-high heat. Season the chicken with ½ teaspoon salt and ¼ teaspoon pepper and cook until browned, 6 to 7 minutes per side; transfer to a plate.

▶ Spoon off and discard the fat. Return the pot to medium-high heat, add the broth, and scrape up any brown bits.

▶ Add the radishes, carrots, and sugar to the pot. Place the chicken on top of the vegetables and gently simmer, partially covered, until it is cooked through, 15 to 20 minutes. Sprinkle with the chives.

TIP
Patience is key when browning chicken. It's ready to be turned when it releases easily from the pan (don't tug). Turn it too soon and you interrupt the caramelizing process and risk tearing the skin.

Havarti-stuffed chicken breasts with tomato salad

hands-on time: 20 minutes / total time: 20 minutes / serves 4

4 6-ounce boneless, skinless chicken breasts
4 ounces dill Havarti, cut into small pieces
   Kosher salt and black pepper
3 tablespoons olive oil
1 pound heirloom tomatoes, sliced
4 pepperoncini peppers, thinly sliced

▶ Cut a 2-inch pocket in the thickest part of each chicken breast. Dividing evenly, stuff the pockets with the Havarti. Season the chicken with ½ teaspoon salt and ¼ teaspoon black pepper.

▶ Heat 1 tablespoon of the oil in a large skillet over medium-high heat. Cook the chicken until golden brown and cooked through, 6 to 8 minutes per side.

▶ Serve the chicken with the tomatoes and pepperoncini. Drizzle the vegetables with the remaining 2 tablespoons of oil and season with ½ teaspoon salt and ¼ teaspoon black pepper.

TIP
Don't overstuff the chicken breasts or press down on them during cooking. The cheese will drip into the skillet, making cooking difficult and cleanup messy.

spiced chicken with couscous salad

hands-on time: 10 minutes / total time: 25 minutes / serves 4

3 tablespoons olive oil

4 6-ounce boneless, skinless
   chicken breasts

1 tablespoon paprika

2 teaspoons ground cumin
   Kosher salt and black pepper

3/4 cup couscous

3/4 pound cherry or grape
   tomatoes, quartered

1/4 pound snap peas, thinly sliced
   crosswise (about 1 cup)

1/2 cup torn fresh basil leaves

1/2 teaspoon grated lemon zest
   plus 2 tablespoons fresh
   lemon juice

▶ Heat 1 tablespoon of the oil in a large skillet over medium heat. Season the chicken with the paprika, cumin, 1/2 teaspoon salt, and 1/4 teaspoon pepper. Cook until browned and cooked through, 6 to 7 minutes per side. Let the chicken rest for at least 5 minutes before slicing.

▶ Meanwhile, place the couscous in a large bowl. Add 1 cup hot tap water, cover, and let sit for 5 minutes; fluff with a fork. Add the tomatoes, snap peas, basil, lemon zest and juice, the remaining 2 tablespoons of oil, 1/2 teaspoon salt, and 1/4 teaspoon pepper and toss to combine. Serve with the chicken.

TIP
No need to spend time removing the strings from the snap peas for this salad. Cutting the peas into small pieces will keep the fibers from being a nuisance.

spicy orange-glazed drumsticks with green beans

hands-on time: 15 minutes / total time: 45 minutes / serves 4

¼ cup orange marmalade
½ teaspoon Asian chili-garlic sauce
8 chicken drumsticks (about 2½ pounds total)
Kosher salt and black pepper
1 pound green beans, trimmed
1 tablespoon unsalted butter
4 corn muffins, warmed

▶ Heat oven to 400° F. In a small bowl, combine the marmalade and chili-garlic sauce.

▶ Place the chicken on a foil-lined rimmed baking sheet and season with ½ teaspoon salt and ¼ teaspoon pepper. Roast until cooked through, 35 to 40 minutes, brushing occasionally with the marmalade mixture during the last 10 minutes of cooking.

▶ Meanwhile, bring a pot of salted water to a boil. Cook the green beans until tender, 4 to 6 minutes. Drain and toss with the butter and ¼ teaspoon each salt and pepper. Serve with the chicken and muffins.

TIP
If you don't have orange marmalade, use apricot preserves or apple jelly instead.

chicken and prosciutto club sandwiches

hands-on time: 20 minutes / total time: 20 minutes / serves 4

8 thin slices prosciutto
1 tablespoon olive oil
4 small chicken cutlets
   (about $3/4$ pound total)
   Kosher salt and black pepper
4 sandwich rolls
$1/4$ cup mayonnaise
$1/4$ cup olive tapenade
1 medium tomato, sliced
$1/2$ cup baby arugula

▶ Heat oven to 400° F. Place the prosciutto in a single layer on a rimmed baking sheet and bake until crisp, 8 to 10 minutes.

▶ Meanwhile, heat the oil in a large skillet over medium-high heat. Season the chicken with ½ teaspoon salt and ¼ teaspoon pepper and cook until golden brown and cooked through, 2 to 3 minutes per side.

▶ Form sandwiches with the rolls, mayonnaise, tapenade, chicken, prosciutto, tomato, and arugula.

TIP
If you don't have tapenade, mix chopped black olives into the mayonnaise.

roasted chicken with carrots and potatoes

hands-on time: 25 minutes / total time: 1½ hours / serves 4

1½ pounds new potatoes
   (about 20)
1 pound medium carrots
   (about 6), halved lengthwise
   and cut into 2-inch pieces
2 tablespoons olive oil
   Kosher salt and black pepper
1 lemon
8 sprigs fresh thyme
1 3½- to 4-pound chicken,
   patted dry
2 tablespoons unsalted butter,
   at room temperature

▶ Heat oven to 425° F. Place the potatoes and carrots in a large roasting pan or baking dish and toss with the oil, ½ teaspoon salt, and ¼ teaspoon pepper.

▶ Pierce the lemon several times with a knife and place it and the thyme in the cavity of the chicken. Rub the chicken with the butter and season with ½ teaspoon salt and ¼ teaspoon pepper. Tie the legs together with kitchen twine, if desired, and nestle the chicken in the vegetables.

▶ Roast until the vegetables are tender, the chicken is golden brown, and its juices run clear when the thigh is pierced with a fork, 65 to 75 minutes (an instant-read thermometer should register 165° F when inserted in the thickest part of the thigh). Let the chicken rest for at least 10 minutes before carving. Serve with the vegetables.

TIP
Find carving a bird a challenge? Use kitchen shears instead of a knife.

crispy turkey cutlets with green bean salad

hands-on time: 25 minutes / total time: 25 minutes / serves 4

¾ pound green beans, trimmed

1 cup grape tomatoes, halved

½ cup pitted kalamata olives, quartered

1 tablespoon fresh lemon juice, plus lemon wedges for serving

4 tablespoons olive oil
Kosher salt and black pepper

¼ cup all-purpose flour

2 large eggs, beaten

⅔ cup bread crumbs

4 thin turkey cutlets (about 1 pound total)

▶ In a large saucepan fitted with a steamer basket, bring 1 inch of water to a boil. Place the green beans in the basket, cover, and steam until tender, 4 to 5 minutes. Run under cold water to cool.

▶ In a large bowl, toss the green beans, tomatoes, and olives with the lemon juice, 1 tablespoon of the oil, and ¼ teaspoon each salt and pepper.

▶ Place the flour, eggs, and bread crumbs in separate shallow bowls. Season the turkey with ½ teaspoon salt and ¼ teaspoon pepper. Coat with the flour (tapping off any excess), dip in the eggs (shaking off any excess), then coat with the bread crumbs, pressing gently to help them adhere.

▶ Heat the remaining 3 tablespoons of oil in a large skillet over medium-high heat. Cook the turkey until golden and cooked through, 2 to 3 minutes per side. Serve with the salad and lemon wedges.

TIP
The green beans can be cooked and the cutlets breaded up to a day in advance; refrigerate, covered, separately. Cook the cutlets and finish the salad just before serving.

chicken and chorizo tostadas

hands-on time: 15 minutes / total time: 15 minutes / serves 4

1 tablespoon olive oil

4 small chicken cutlets
(about ¾ pound total)
Kosher salt and black pepper

4 small flour tortillas

4 ounces cured chorizo, thinly
sliced

8 ounces Cheddar, grated
(2 cups)

¼ cup fresh cilantro leaves

¼ cup sour cream

▶ Heat broiler. Heat the oil in a large skillet over medium-high heat. Season the chicken with ½ teaspoon salt and ¼ teaspoon pepper and cook until golden brown and cooked through, 2 to 3 minutes per side. Cut into strips.

▶ Place the tortillas on a broilerproof rimmed baking sheet and broil until crisp, about 1 minute. Dividing evenly, top with the chicken, chorizo, and Cheddar. Broil until the cheese melts. Sprinkle with the cilantro and serve with the sour cream.

TIP
Cured chorizo, also called Spanish chorizo, is a flavorful pork sausage seasoned with garlic and paprika. Try it in stews, omelets, or seafood pilafs.

chicken with spinach and mushrooms

hands-on time: 20 minutes / total time: 25 minutes / serves 4

2 tablespoons olive oil

4 6-ounce boneless, skinless chicken breasts
  Kosher salt and black pepper

1 pound button mushrooms, quartered

1 red bell pepper, cut into ¹/₂-inch pieces

2 cloves garlic, chopped

¹/₂ cup dry white wine

2 bunches flat-leaf spinach, thick stems removed (about 8 cups)

▶ Heat 1 tablespoon of the oil in a large skillet over medium-high heat. Season the chicken with ½ teaspoon salt and ¼ teaspoon black pepper. Cook until browned and cooked through, 5 to 7 minutes per side; transfer to plates.

▶ Return the skillet to medium-high heat and heat the remaining tablespoon of oil. Cook the mushrooms and bell pepper, tossing, for 3 minutes. Add the garlic and wine and cook until the mushrooms are tender and the wine is nearly evaporated, 2 to 3 minutes more.

▶ Add the spinach and ½ teaspoon each salt and black pepper to the vegetables and toss to combine. Serve with the chicken.

TIP
For even richer flavor, cook 2 slices of bacon (cut into pieces) in the skillet before adding the mushrooms and bell pepper.

Thai red curry chicken

hands-on time: 20 minutes / total time: 20 minutes / serves 4

1 cup long-grain white rice

2 tablespoons canola oil

8 small chicken cutlets (about 1½ pounds total)

   Kosher salt and black pepper

2 red bell peppers, sliced

2 tablespoons red curry paste

1 15-ounce can coconut milk

1 lime, cut into wedges

¼ cup torn fresh basil leaves

▶ Cook the rice according to the package directions.

▶ Meanwhile, heat the oil in a large skillet over medium-high heat. Season the chicken with ½ teaspoon salt and ¼ teaspoon black pepper. In batches, cook the chicken until golden brown and cooked through, 2 to 3 minutes per side; remove from the skillet and cut into strips.

▶ Add the bell peppers and ¼ cup water to the skillet and cook, tossing frequently, until just tender, 3 to 4 minutes. Add the curry paste and coconut milk and simmer until slightly thickened, 3 to 5 minutes. Add the chicken and toss to combine.

▶ Serve the chicken curry over the rice with the lime wedges and sprinkle with the basil.

TIP
Canola oil has a neutral taste and a high smoke point (meaning it can get very hot without burning). This makes it a good choice for Asian stir-fries.

dinner tonight:
beef & lamb

grilled beef and pepper fajitas

hands-on time: 20 minutes / total time: 20 minutes / serves 4

1 pound flank steak
1 teaspoon ground cumin
  Kosher salt and black pepper
1 red bell pepper, sliced
  ½ inch thick
1 yellow bell pepper, sliced
  ½ inch thick
1 tablespoon olive oil
8 small flour tortillas
1 avocado, sliced
½ cup sour cream
  Hot sauce (optional)

▶ Heat grill to medium-high. Season the beef with the cumin, ½ teaspoon salt, and ¼ teaspoon black pepper.

▶ In a large bowl, toss the bell peppers with the oil and ¼ teaspoon each salt and black pepper.

▶ Grill the beef to the desired doneness, 4 to 5 minutes per side for medium-rare. Let rest for at least 5 minutes before slicing.

▶ Meanwhile, grill the peppers, turning occasionally, until tender, 8 to 10 minutes.

▶ Fill the tortillas with the beef, peppers, and avocado. Serve with the sour cream and the hot sauce, if desired.

TIP
Slice the meat across the grain to break up chewy fibers and make it more tender.

Gouda cheeseburgers with fennel-onion relish

hands-on time: 30 minutes / total time: 30 minutes / serves 4

2 pounds medium sweet potatoes (about 4), peeled and cut into 1/2-inch wedges

3 tablespoons plus 1 teaspoon olive oil
Kosher salt and black pepper

1/2 small fennel bulb, cored and thinly sliced

1/2 small red onion, thinly sliced

3 tablespoons fresh lemon juice

1 1/4 pounds ground beef chuck

4 ounces Gouda, sliced

4 hamburger buns
Arugula, for serving

▶ Heat oven to 450° F. On a rimmed baking sheet, toss the potatoes with 2 tablespoons of the oil, 3/4 teaspoon salt, and 1/4 teaspoon pepper. Roast, tossing once, until golden brown and tender, 22 to 25 minutes.

▶ Meanwhile, in a medium bowl, toss the fennel and onion with the lemon juice, 1 tablespoon of the remaining oil, and 1/4 teaspoon each salt and pepper; set aside.

▶ Form the beef into four 1/2-inch-thick patties and season with 1/2 teaspoon salt and 1/4 teaspoon pepper. Heat the remaining teaspoon of oil in a large skillet over medium-high heat. Cook the patties to the desired doneness, 3 to 5 minutes per side for medium. During the last minute of cooking, top the burgers with the Gouda and cook, covered.

▶ Place the burgers on the buns with the arugula and fennel-onion relish. Serve with the fries.

TIP
Sweet potatoes have tender, edible skin. If you scrub them well, you don't have to peel them for this recipe.

grilled steak, plums, and bok choy

hands-on time: 20 minutes / total time: 40 minutes / serves 4

1½ pounds flank steak
¼ cup low-sodium soy sauce
4 plums, cut into wedges
4 heads baby bok choy, halved
    lengthwise
1 tablespoon canola oil
    Kosher salt and black pepper
2 teaspoons toasted sesame
    seeds

▶ Place the steak and soy sauce in a shallow dish and toss to coat. Let the steak marinate, turning occasionally, for at least 15 minutes.

▶ Meanwhile, heat grill to medium-high. In a large bowl, toss the plums and bok choy with the oil, ½ teaspoon salt, and ¼ teaspoon pepper.

▶ Grill the steak to the desired doneness, 4 to 6 minutes per side for medium-rare. Let rest for at least 5 minutes before slicing.

▶ Meanwhile, grill the plums and bok choy until tender, about 2 minutes per side. Serve with the steak and sprinkle with the sesame seeds.

TIP
To enhance the sesame flavor, drizzle the bok choy and plums with a little toasted sesame oil just before serving.

59

lamb chops with curried rice and cherries

hands-on time: 25 minutes / total time: 25 minutes / serves 4

1 cup long-grain white rice
1 teaspoon curry powder
1 cup cherries, halved and
   pitted
½ cup torn fresh basil leaves
1 teaspoon olive oil
8 small lamb rib or loin chops
   (¾ inch thick; about
   2 pounds total)
   Kosher salt and black pepper

▶ Cook the rice according to the package directions, adding the curry powder to the water before cooking. Gently fold the cherries and basil into the cooked rice.

▶ Meanwhile, heat the oil in a large skillet over medium-high heat. Season the lamb with ½ teaspoon salt and ¼ teaspoon pepper. In batches, cook the lamb to the desired doneness, 2 to 4 minutes per side for medium-rare, adding more oil to the pan if necessary. Serve with the rice.

TIP
Turn this meal into a salad the next day. Slice the lamb and serve it, along with the rice, over greens drizzled with your favorite vinaigrette.

steak with potato salad and blue cheese vinaigrette

hands-on time: 15 minutes / total time: 30 minutes / serves 4

1 pound red new potatoes
(about 12)
Kosher salt and black pepper

¼ cup plus 1 tablespoon
olive oil

4 small steaks (such as
Newport, flat iron, or
top round; 1 inch thick;
about 1½ pounds total)

1 ounce blue cheese, crumbled
(¼ cup)

2 tablespoons white wine
vinegar

1 small head Boston lettuce,
torn (about 4 cups)

▶ Place the potatoes in a large saucepan and add enough cold water to cover. Bring to a boil and add 2 teaspoons salt. Reduce heat and simmer until tender, 14 to 16 minutes. Drain, run under cold water to cool, and using a fork, break the potatoes in half.

▶ Meanwhile, heat 1 tablespoon of the oil in a large skillet over medium-high heat. Season the steaks with 1 teaspoon salt and ¾ teaspoon pepper and cook to the desired doneness, 4 to 5 minutes per side for medium-rare.

▶ In a large bowl, combine the blue cheese, vinegar, the remaining ¼ cup of oil, ½ teaspoon salt, and ¼ teaspoon pepper. Add the lettuce and potatoes and toss to coat. Serve with the steaks.

TIP
Any type of blue cheese will work with this vinaigrette. Try spicy Maytag Blue, earthy Stilton, creamy Gorgonzola, or salty, strong-flavored Roquefort.

slow-cooker corned beef, Brussels sprouts, and carrots

hands-on time: 15 minutes / total time: 4 to 8 hours / serves 4 (with leftovers)

1 pound carrots, cut into
   3-inch pieces
1 12-ounce bottle amber ale
1 3-pound piece corned beef
   brisket (with spice packet,
   if included)
¾ pound Brussels sprouts
½ cup sour cream
2 tablespoons whole-grain
   mustard
1 tablespoon chopped fresh
   tarragon

▶ In a 5- to 6-quart slow cooker, combine the carrots, amber ale, and contents of the spice packet (if included). Nestle the beef in the carrots and cook, covered, until tender, on high for 4 to 5 hours or on low for 7 to 8 hours.

▶ Ten minutes before serving, thinly slice the Brussels sprouts. (This is easiest to do in a food processor fitted with the slicing blade.)

▶ Transfer the beef to a cutting board. If the slow cooker is on the low setting, turn it to high. Add the Brussels sprouts to the carrots in the slow cooker and cook, covered, until the Brussels sprouts are tender, 4 to 6 minutes.

▶ Meanwhile, in a small bowl, combine the sour cream, mustard, and tarragon.

▶ Slice the beef and serve with the vegetables and sour cream sauce.

TIP
Corned beef brisket sold in the supermarket meat case is uncooked, unlike the cooked corned beef at the deli counter. Brisket that comes without a packet of spices has already been cured.

deep-dish cheeseburger pizza

hands-on time: 15 minutes / total time: 35 minutes / serves 4

1 tablespoon plus 1 teaspoon
  olive oil, plus more for
  the skillet
½ pound ground beef
¼ cup barbecue sauce
1 pound pizza dough, thawed
  if frozen
4 ounces Cheddar, grated
  (1 cup)
1 cup baby arugula
1 small tomato, sliced
¼ small red onion, thinly sliced
  Kosher salt and black pepper

▶ Heat oven to 425° F. Heat 1 teaspoon of the oil in a large skillet over medium-high heat. Add the beef and cook, breaking it up with a spoon, until no longer pink, 4 to 5 minutes. Stir in the barbecue sauce.

▶ Oil a 10-inch ovenproof skillet. Press the dough into the bottom and up the sides. Top the dough with the beef and sprinkle with the Cheddar. Bake until golden brown, 20 to 25 minutes.

▶ Top the pizza with the arugula, tomato, and onion. Drizzle with the remaining tablespoon of oil and sprinkle with a pinch each of salt and pepper.

TIP
If you don't have a 10-inch oven-proof skillet, use a 9-inch cake pan.

spicy beef kebabs with minted watermelon salad

hands-on time: 20 minutes / total time: 20 minutes / serves 4

2 pounds watermelon (about $1/4$ medium), rind removed, cut into pieces

$1/4$ red onion, thinly sliced

$1/2$ cup torn fresh mint leaves
Kosher salt and black pepper

$1\frac{1}{2}$ pounds tri-tip or sirloin steak, cut into $1\frac{1}{2}$-inch pieces

8 red jalapeño peppers, sliced into 1-inch-thick rings

1 lime, cut into wedges

▶ Soak 8 wooden skewers for 10 minutes. Heat grill to medium-high.

▶ Meanwhile, arrange the watermelon on a platter. Sprinkle with the onion, mint, and $1/4$ teaspoon each salt and black pepper; set aside.

▶ Thread the beef and jalapeños onto the skewers and season with $1/2$ teaspoon each salt and black pepper. Grill, turning frequently, to the desired doneness, 6 to 8 minutes for medium-rare.

▶ Serve with the lime wedges and watermelon salad.

TIP
Before buying a precut piece of watermelon, look closely. Cut sides with flesh that appears mealy or is separating from the seeds indicate that the fruit is old.

lamb with golden Israeli couscous

hands-on time: 15 minutes / total time: 25 minutes / serves 4

2 tablespoons olive oil

3 lamb shoulder chops (1 inch thick; about 2 pounds total)

1 teaspoon paprika

½ teaspoon ground cinnamon Kosher salt and black pepper

1 medium onion, chopped

1¼ cups Israeli couscous (also labeled "pearl couscous")

½ cup dried apricots, quartered

1 large pinch saffron (optional)

4 cups baby spinach (about 4 ounces)

▶ Heat 1 tablespoon of the oil in a large skillet over medium-high heat. Season the lamb with the paprika, cinnamon, ½ teaspoon salt, and ¼ teaspoon pepper and cook to the desired doneness, 4 to 6 minutes per side for medium-rare. Let rest for at least 5 minutes before slicing.

▶ Meanwhile, heat the remaining tablespoon of oil in a medium saucepan over medium-high heat. Add the onion and cook, stirring occasionally, until softened, 3 to 4 minutes.

▶ Add the couscous, apricots, saffron (if desired), 1 teaspoon salt, ¼ teaspoon pepper, and 2 cups water to the saucepan, stir, and bring to a boil. Reduce heat and gently simmer, covered, until the couscous is tender and the water is absorbed, 8 to 10 minutes. Fold in the spinach and serve with the lamb.

TIP
Israeli couscous looks like a grain but is really a pearl-shaped pasta that is toasted, giving it a slightly nutty flavor. Like conventional couscous, it is delicious served hot or at room temperature. For a cool summer salad, toss it with olive oil, cucumbers, Feta, and mint.

sweet and spicy beef stir-fry

hands-on time: 20 minutes / total time: 20 minutes / serves 4

8 ounces lo mein noodles

1 tablespoon canola oil

1 pound flank steak, thinly sliced across the grain
  Kosher salt and black pepper

½ pound snow peas, halved lengthwise

2 medium carrots, thinly sliced

2 shallots, sliced

⅓ cup red pepper jelly

▶ Cook the noodles according to the package directions.

▶ Meanwhile, heat the oil in a large skillet over medium-high heat. Season the beef with ½ teaspoon salt and ¼ teaspoon pepper and cook, tossing occasionally, until cooked through, 3 to 4 minutes; transfer to a plate.

▶ Add the snow peas, carrots, and shallots to the skillet and cook, tossing occasionally, for 4 minutes.

▶ Return the beef to the skillet, add the jelly, and cook, tossing, for 1 minute. Serve with the noodles.

TIP
To make the meat easier to slice thinly, firm it up first in the freezer for 10 to 15 minutes.

dinner tonight:
pork

roasted pork chops and peaches

hands-on time: 20 minutes / total time: 30 minutes / serves 4

1 10-ounce package couscous (1½ cups)

1 tablespoon olive oil

4 bone-in pork chops (¾ inch thick; about 2 pounds total)
   Kosher salt and black pepper

2 peaches, cut into wedges

1 small red onion, cut into thin wedges

3 tablespoons white wine vinegar

½ cup fresh basil leaves

▶ Heat oven to 400° F. Cook the couscous according to the package directions.

▶ Meanwhile, heat the oil in a large ovenproof skillet over medium-high heat. Season the pork with ½ teaspoon salt and ¼ teaspoon pepper and cook until browned, 3 to 5 minutes per side. Transfer to a plate.

▶ Add the peaches, onion, vinegar, and ¼ teaspoon each salt and pepper to the skillet and cook, tossing, for 1 minute. Return the pork and any accumulated juices to the skillet.

▶ Transfer the skillet to oven and roast until the pork is cooked through and the peaches are tender, 8 to 10 minutes. Serve with the couscous and sprinkle with the basil.

TIP
Nectarines or plums also work nicely in this recipe.

meatballs with pine nuts and raisins

hands-on time: 25 minutes / total time: 25 minutes / serves 4

1¼ pounds ground pork
¼ cup pine nuts
¼ cup chopped raisins or
   currants
¼ teaspoon ground cinnamon
   Kosher salt and black pepper
1 tablespoon olive oil
2 cloves garlic, thinly sliced
2 bunches Swiss chard, thick
   stems removed and leaves
   cut into 2-inch strips (about
   12 cups)
1 small baguette, sliced

▶ Heat broiler. In a large bowl, combine the pork, pine nuts, raisins, cinnamon, 1 teaspoon salt, and ¼ teaspoon pepper.

▶ Form the pork mixture into 20 walnut-size meatballs and place on a foil-lined rimmed baking sheet. Broil, turning once, until cooked through, 6 to 8 minutes.

▶ Meanwhile, heat the oil in a large saucepan over medium heat. Add the garlic and cook, stirring, until golden, 1 to 2 minutes. Add the chard, ½ teaspoon salt, and ¼ teaspoon pepper and cook, tossing occasionally, until wilted, 3 to 4 minutes more. Serve with the meatballs and bread.

TIP
Shaping meatballs can be sticky business. Wet your hands with cold water first (and repeat as needed) to keep things clean.

tapas plate with marinated chickpeas

hands-on time: 15 minutes / total time: 15 minutes / serves 4

1 15.5-ounce can chickpeas, rinsed

½ cup raisins

¼ cup chopped roasted red peppers

¼ cup chopped fresh flat-leaf parsley

2 scallions, sliced

3 tablespoons olive oil
  Kosher salt and black pepper

½ pound manchego, sliced

¼ pound thinly sliced Serrano ham or prosciutto

½ cup mixed olives

½ small loaf country bread

▶ In a medium bowl, toss the chickpeas, raisins, roasted red peppers, parsley, and scallions with the oil, ½ teaspoon salt, and ¼ teaspoon black pepper.

▶ Serve with the manchego, ham, olives, and bread.

TIP
This chickpea mixture is also delicious served over greens for a hearty main-course salad.

gingery pork and cucumber pitas

hands-on time: 15 minutes / total time: 15 minutes / serves 4

¼ cup rice vinegar
2 teaspoons sugar
   Kosher salt
2 Kirby cucumbers, thinly sliced
1 red or green jalapeño pepper, thinly sliced and seeded, if desired, for less heat
1 tablespoon olive oil
1 pound ground pork
¼ cup hoisin sauce
1 tablespoon grated fresh ginger
4 pitas, halved

▶ In a medium bowl, combine the vinegar, sugar, and ¼ teaspoon salt; stir until the sugar dissolves. Add the cucumbers and jalapeño and let sit, tossing occasionally, for at least 5 minutes.

▶ Meanwhile, heat the oil in a large skillet over medium-high heat. Cook the pork, breaking it up with a spoon, until no longer pink, 5 to 6 minutes. Stir in the hoisin, ginger, and 2 tablespoons water.

▶ Dividing evenly, fill the pita halves with the pork and the cucumber salad.

TIP
Try this refreshing cucumber salad in a ham sandwich or as a burger topping.

pork chops with garlicky broccoli

hands-on time: 20 minutes / total time: 20 minutes / serves 4

1 cup long-grain white rice

3 tablespoons olive oil

4 bone-in pork chops (1 inch thick; about 2½ pounds total)

Kosher salt and black pepper

1 bunch broccoli, cut into florets

2 cloves garlic, chopped

2 tablespoons low-sodium soy sauce

▶ Heat oven to 400° F. Cook the rice according to the package directions.

▶ Meanwhile, heat 1 tablespoon of the oil in a large ovenproof skillet over medium-high heat. Season the pork with ½ teaspoon salt and ¼ teaspoon pepper and cook until browned, 2 to 3 minutes per side. Transfer the skillet to oven and roast the pork until cooked through, 6 to 8 minutes.

▶ Meanwhile, heat the remaining 2 tablespoons of oil in a second large skillet over medium-high heat. Add the broccoli, garlic, soy sauce, and ⅓ cup water. Cook, covered, until the broccoli is tender, 5 to 6 minutes. Serve with the pork and rice.

TIP
For fluffier rice, before cooking, rinse the grains in a sieve under cold water until the water runs clear.

apricot-glazed ham with potatoes and asparagus

hands-on time: 15 minutes / total time: 1 hour / serves 4 (with leftover ham)

1 3-pound boneless ham
¼ cup apricot preserves
1 pound fingerling or some
  other small potatoes
  (about 12)
  Kosher salt and black pepper
1 pound asparagus, cut into
  1-inch pieces
3 tablespoons olive oil
1 tablespoon white wine
  vinegar
1 tablespoon prepared
  horseradish
¼ cup fresh dill sprigs

▶ Heat oven to 350° F. Place the ham on a foil-lined rimmed baking sheet and cook until heated through, 50 to 60 minutes, spreading the ham with the preserves after 20 minutes of cooking.

▶ Meanwhile, place the potatoes in a large saucepan and add enough cold water to cover. Bring to a boil and add 1 teaspoon salt. Reduce heat and simmer until tender, 15 to 18 minutes.

▶ With a slotted spoon, transfer the potatoes to a colander. Run under cold water to cool, then cut into quarters.

▶ Return the water in the saucepan to a boil. Add the asparagus and cook until tender, 2 to 3 minutes. Drain and run under cold water to cool.

▶ In a large bowl, whisk together the oil, vinegar, horseradish, ½ teaspoon salt, and ¼ teaspoon pepper. Add the potatoes and asparagus and toss to combine; fold in the dill. Thinly slice the ham and serve with the vegetables.

TIP
To keep leftover ham from drying out, slice only what you will use for dinner and wrap the rest. The ham will last for up to 4 days in the refrigerator. Reheat, if desired, and slice just before serving.

ham, Gruyère, and shallot pizza

hands-on time: 15 minutes / **total time: 50 minutes** / **serves 6**

1 pound pizza dough, thawed
if frozen
Cornmeal, for the pan

2 tablespoons olive oil

2 shallots, sliced into thin rings

12 sprigs fresh thyme
Kosher salt and black pepper

½ pound thinly sliced cooked
ham

2 ounces Gruyère or Swiss
cheese, grated (½ cup)

▶ Heat oven to 425° F. Shape the dough into a 14-inch round and place on a cornmeal-dusted rimmed baking sheet.

▶ Brush the dough with 1 tablespoon of the oil and bake until puffed and golden, 15 to 20 minutes.

▶ Meanwhile, in a medium bowl, toss the shallots and thyme with the remaining tablespoon of oil and ¼ teaspoon each salt and pepper.

▶ Top the partially cooked dough with the ham, shallot mixture, and Gruyère. Bake until the crust is crisp and the cheese has melted, 12 to 15 minutes.

TIP
To thaw frozen pizza dough quickly, place it in a resealable plastic bag and set it in a bowl of cold water for 10 to 20 minutes.

paprika-spiced pork chops with spinach sauté

hands-on time: 20 minutes / total time: 25 minutes / serves 4

1 tablespoon olive oil
4 bone-in pork chops (1 inch thick; about 2½ pounds total)
1 teaspoon paprika
   Kosher salt and black pepper
4 scallions, sliced
¼ cup golden raisins
1 10-ounce package spinach, thick stems removed (about 16 loosely packed cups)
1 tablespoon fresh lemon juice

▶ Heat oven to 400° F. Heat the oil in a large skillet over medium-high heat. Season the pork with the paprika, ½ teaspoon salt, and ¼ teaspoon pepper and cook until browned, 2 to 3 minutes per side.

▶ Transfer the pork to a rimmed baking sheet and roast until cooked through, 10 to 12 minutes.

▶ Meanwhile, return the skillet to medium heat, add the scallions and raisins, and cook, stirring, for 30 seconds. Add the spinach and ¼ teaspoon each salt and pepper and cook, tossing, until just wilted, 1 to 2 minutes more. Stir in the lemon juice. Serve with the pork.

TIP
To add a touch of smoky flavor, substitute smoked paprika (often labeled "pimentón") for the usual sweet variety.

brown sugar–glazed pork with grilled corn

hands-on time: 15 minutes / total time: 35 minutes / serves 4

¼ cup Worcestershire sauce
2 tablespoons brown sugar
1 pork tenderloin (about
    1¼ pounds)
   Kosher salt and black pepper
4 ears corn, shucked
2 tablespoons unsalted butter
2 scallions, sliced

▶ Heat grill to medium-high. In a small bowl, mix together the Worcestershire sauce and brown sugar.

▶ Season the pork with ½ teaspoon salt and ¼ teaspoon pepper. Grill, turning often, until the internal temperature registers 145° F, 20 to 25 minutes, brushing with the brown sugar glaze during the last 5 minutes of cooking. Let rest for at least 5 minutes before slicing.

▶ Meanwhile, grill the corn, turning occasionally, until tender and slightly charred, 6 to 8 minutes. Cut the kernels off the cobs into a medium bowl and toss with the butter, scallions, ½ teaspoon salt, and ¼ teaspoon pepper. Serve with the pork.

TIP
When cutting corn off the cob, stand the cob on end in a wide, shallow bowl or on a rimmed baking sheet to catch the kernels and juices.

dinner tonight:
seafood

salmon with brown butter, almonds, and green beans

hands-on time: 20 minutes / total time: 20 minutes / serves 4

4 tablespoons unsalted butter
1¼ pounds skinless salmon
 fillet, cut into 4 pieces
 Kosher salt and black pepper
1 pound green beans, trimmed
 and halved crosswise
¼ cup sliced almonds
2 tablespoons capers

▶ Heat 1 tablespoon of the butter in a large nonstick skillet over medium heat. Season the salmon with ½ teaspoon salt and ¼ teaspoon pepper. Cook until opaque throughout, 3 to 5 minutes per side; transfer to plates.

▶ Meanwhile, fill a second large skillet with ½ inch of water, bring to a boil, and add ¼ teaspoon salt. Add the green beans, cover, and cook until just tender, 4 to 5 minutes; drain and transfer to plates.

▶ Wipe out the second skillet and heat the remaining 3 tablespoons of butter over medium heat. Add the almonds and cook, stirring frequently, until both the almonds and the butter are golden brown (but not burned), 2 to 3 minutes. Stir in the capers. Spoon over the salmon and green beans.

TIP
The green beans with brown butter and almonds make an easy, impressive side dish for almost anything. Try them with roasted chicken or grilled steak.

mussels with pesto and garlic oven fries

hands-on time: 15 minutes / total time: 40 minutes / serves 4

2 pounds russet potatoes
(about 4 medium), cut into
$\frac{1}{4}$-inch-thick sticks

4 garlic cloves, smashed

2 tablespoons olive oil
Kosher salt and black pepper

1 cup dry white wine

2 pounds mussels, scrubbed

$\frac{1}{2}$ cup pesto

▶ Heat oven to 425° F. On a rimmed baking sheet, toss the potatoes and garlic with the oil, $\frac{3}{4}$ teaspoon salt, and $\frac{1}{4}$ teaspoon pepper.

▶ Roast the potatoes, turning once, until golden brown and crisp, 30 to 35 minutes.

▶ When the potatoes have 5 minutes left to cook, in a large pot bring the wine to a boil. Add the mussels and simmer, covered, until they open, 3 to 4 minutes. (Discard any that remain closed.) Transfer the mussels to bowls. Mix the pesto into the cooking liquid and spoon over the mussels. Serve with the oven fries.

TIP
Dry vermouth is a tasty substitute for white wine in this and other recipes. Try it the next time you want to avoid opening a bottle of white wine for cooking. (An opened bottle of vermouth will last for months in the refrigerator.)

ancho-rubbed salmon with summer squash

hands-on time: 20 minutes / total time: 20 minutes / serves 4

1 tablespoon brown sugar

1½ teaspoons ground ancho chili pepper

Kosher salt and black pepper

1¼ pounds skinless salmon fillet, cut into 4 pieces

2 tablespoons olive oil

1½ pounds small summer squash (about 4), thinly sliced

2 scallions, sliced

▶ Heat oven to 400° F. In a small bowl, combine the brown sugar, ancho chili, and ½ teaspoon salt.

▶ Place the salmon on a foil-lined rimmed baking sheet and drizzle with 1 tablespoon of the oil. Rub with the sugar mixture and roast until opaque throughout, 12 to 15 minutes.

▶ Meanwhile, heat the remaining tablespoon of oil in a large skillet over medium-high heat. Add the squash, ½ teaspoon salt, and ¼ teaspoon black pepper and cook, tossing occasionally, until just tender and beginning to brown, 5 to 7 minutes. Fold in the scallions. Serve with the salmon.

TIP
Take this recipe outside in summer. Grill the squash (halved lengthwise) and the salmon over medium-high heat until the squash is tender and the salmon is opaque throughout, 3 to 5 minutes per side. Slice the squash and toss with the scallions, oil, salt, and pepper.

curried shrimp rolls

hands-on time: 10 minutes / total time: 10 minutes / serves 4

¼ cup mayonnaise
1 tablespoon fresh lemon juice
¾ teaspoon curry powder
   Kosher salt and black pepper
1 pound cooked peeled and
   deveined large shrimp,
   coarsely chopped
2 stalks celery, chopped
1 cup chopped arugula
4 hot dog buns, toasted

▶ In a medium bowl, whisk together the mayonnaise, lemon juice, curry powder, and ¼ teaspoon each salt and pepper.

▶ Add the shrimp, celery, and arugula to the bowl and toss to combine. Serve in the buns.

TIP
If you're feeling indulgent, butter the buns inside and out and cook in a skillet, pressing occasionally, until golden brown.

seared scallops with snow peas and orange

hands-on time: 25 minutes / total time: 25 minutes / serves 4

1 cup couscous

1 tablespoon plus 2 teaspoons
   olive oil

16 sea scallops (about 1½ pounds)
   Kosher salt and black pepper

4 strips orange zest (removed
   with a vegetable peeler),
   thinly sliced

¾ pound snow peas, trimmed
   and halved lengthwise

▶ Cook the couscous according to the package directions.

▶ Meanwhile, heat 2 teaspoons of the oil in a large nonstick skillet over medium-high heat. Pat the scallops dry, season with ¼ teaspoon each salt and pepper, and cook until opaque throughout, 2 to 3 minutes per side. Transfer to a plate and cover to keep warm. Wipe out the skillet.

▶ Heat the remaining tablespoon of oil in the skillet over medium-high heat. Add the orange zest, snow peas, and ¼ teaspoon each salt and pepper and cook, tossing frequently, until the snow peas are just tender, about 2 minutes. Serve with the scallops and couscous.

TIP
Some scallops arrive in the store with the muscle still attached. A quick tug with your fingers removes it easily.

shrimp and bacon with Cheddar grits

hands-on time: 20 minutes / total time: 20 minutes / serves 4

1 cup grits
4 ounces Cheddar, grated
  (1 cup)
4 slices bacon, cut into
  ½-inch pieces
1 pound peeled and deveined
  medium shrimp
2 plum tomatoes, chopped
2 scallions, sliced

▶ Cook the grits according to the package directions. Stir in the Cheddar.

▶ Meanwhile, cook the bacon in a large skillet over medium heat until crisp, 6 to 8 minutes. With a slotted spoon, transfer to a paper towel–lined plate.

▶ Add the shrimp and tomatoes to the bacon drippings in the skillet and cook, tossing occasionally, until the shrimp are opaque throughout, 3 to 5 minutes. Fold in the scallions and bacon and serve over the grits.

TIP
For a spicy New Orleans accent, try sliced andouille sausage in place of the bacon.

salmon kebabs with cilantro sauce

hands-on time: 15 minutes / total time: 25 minutes / serves 4

2 tablespoons pine nuts
1¼ pounds skinless salmon
    fillet, cut into 1½-inch pieces
    Kosher salt and black pepper
¼ cup olive oil
¼ cup chopped fresh cilantro
2 teaspoons grated lemon zest
4 pieces lavash bread

▶ Soak 16 wooden skewers in water for 10 minutes. Heat grill to medium-high. Heat oven to 350° F.

▶ Spread the pine nuts on a rimmed baking sheet and toast, tossing occasionally, until golden brown, 4 to 6 minutes. Let cool, then chop.

▶ Meanwhile, thread the salmon onto pairs of skewers and season with ½ teaspoon salt and ¼ teaspoon pepper. Grill, turning occasionally, until opaque throughout, 4 to 6 minutes.

▶ In a small bowl, combine the oil, cilantro, lemon zest, and pine nuts. Serve the salmon with the sauce and lavash.

TIP
Using 2 skewers instead of one prevents the salmon from turning and sliding during grilling. Try this with all types of kebabs.

ginger-glazed cod with sautéed summer squash

hands-on time: 10 minutes / total time: 20 minutes / serves 4

2 tablespoons brown sugar

1 tablespoon low-sodium
soy sauce

2 teaspoons grated fresh
ginger

4 6-ounce pieces skinless cod,
halibut, or striped bass fillet

2 tablespoons plus 1 teaspoon
canola oil
Kosher salt and black pepper

1½ pounds small zucchini
and summer squash (about
4 total), thinly sliced

¼ teaspoon crushed red pepper

¼ cup torn fresh mint leaves

▶ Heat broiler. In a small bowl, combine the brown sugar, soy sauce, and ginger; set aside.

▶ Place the cod on a foil-lined broilerproof rimmed baking sheet. Drizzle with 1 teaspoon of the oil and season with ¼ teaspoon each salt and black pepper. Broil until the cod is opaque throughout, 5 to 7 minutes, basting with the soy mixture twice during the last 2 minutes of cooking.

▶ Meanwhile, heat the remaining 2 tablespoons of oil in a large skillet over medium-high heat. Add the zucchini, squash, red pepper, and ½ teaspoon salt and cook, tossing frequently, until just tender, 5 to 7 minutes. Fold in the mint. Serve with the cod.

TIP
Have leftover ginger you won't be using soon? Peel it and pop it in the freezer. The next time you need it, just grate the frozen root. (A rasp grater works best.)

dinner tonight:
pasta

spaghetti with zucchini, walnuts, and raisins

hands-on time: 15 minutes / **total time: 20 minutes** / serves 4

12 ounces spaghetti (¾ box)

3 tablespoons olive oil

½ cup walnut halves, roughly chopped

4 cloves garlic, thinly sliced

1½ pounds small zucchini (4 to 5), halved lengthwise and sliced crosswise

¾ cup raisins
   Kosher salt and black pepper

¼ cup grated Parmesan (1 ounce)

▶ Cook the pasta according to the package directions; drain and return it to the pot.

▶ Meanwhile, heat the oil in a large skillet over medium-high heat. Add the walnuts and cook, stirring frequently, until beginning to brown, 3 to 4 minutes. Add the garlic and cook, stirring, until beginning to brown, about 1 minute.

▶ Add the zucchini and raisins to the skillet, season with ½ teaspoon salt and ¼ teaspoon pepper, and cook, tossing occasionally, until the zucchini is just tender, 4 to 5 minutes.

▶ Add the zucchini mixture to the pasta and toss to combine. Serve with the Parmesan.

TIP
Garlic can rapidly go from golden to scorched. Before placing it in the oil, have the zucchini sliced and ready to go. When the zucchini and raisins hit the pan, they will lower the temperature of the oil and keep the garlic from overcooking.

pasta with chicken sausage and broccoli

hands-on time: 20 minutes / **total time: 20 minutes** / serves 4

12 ounces rigatoni (³/₄ box)
 1 tablespoon olive oil
 1 onion, sliced
 6 ounces fully cooked chicken
    sausage links, sliced
 1 small bunch broccoli, cut
    into florets and stems sliced
¹/₄ cup grated Parmesan
    (1 ounce)

▸ Cook the pasta according to the package directions; drain and return it to the pot.

▸ Meanwhile, heat the oil in a large skillet over medium-high heat. Cook the onion, stirring frequently, until beginning to soften, 2 to 3 minutes. Add the sausage and cook, tossing, until browned, 2 to 3 minutes more.

▸ Add the broccoli and 1¹/₄ cups water to the skillet and simmer, covered, until the broccoli is tender, 5 to 6 minutes.

▸ Add the sausage mixture and Parmesan to the pasta and toss to combine.

TIP
Fully cooked chicken sausage links come in a number of tasty flavors. For this dish, try a roasted garlic or apple variety.

ravioli with peas and crispy bacon

hands-on time: 25 minutes / total time: 25 minutes
serves 4

- 16 to 18 ounces cheese ravioli (fresh or frozen)
- 6 slices bacon
- 2 cloves garlic, sliced
- 1 10-ounce package frozen peas
  Kosher salt and black pepper
- 1 ounce ricotta salata, grated (¼ cup)

▶ Cook the pasta according to the package directions. Reserve ¼ cup of the cooking water and drain the pasta.

▶ Meanwhile, cook the bacon in a large skillet over medium heat until crisp, 6 to 8 minutes. Transfer to a paper towel–lined plate. Let cool, then break into pieces.

▶ Return the skillet to medium heat, add the garlic, and cook, stirring, until golden brown, 1 to 2 minutes. Add the peas and cook until heated through, 2 to 3 minutes.

▶ Add the pasta, the reserved cooking water, ½ teaspoon salt, and ¼ teaspoon pepper and toss. Sprinkle with the bacon and ricotta salata.

ravioli with brown butter and sage

hands-on time: 10 minutes / total time: 25 minutes
serves 4

- 16 to 18 ounces cheese ravioli (fresh or frozen)
- 6 tablespoons unsalted butter (¾ stick)
- ¼ cup pine nuts
- ⅓ cup fresh sage leaves
  Kosher salt and black pepper

▶ Cook the pasta according to the package directions.

▶ Meanwhile, melt the butter in a large skillet over medium heat. Add the pine nuts and sage and cook, stirring occasionally, until the sage is crisp and the butter and pine nuts are browned (but not burned), 6 to 8 minutes.

▶ Add the pasta, ½ teaspoon salt, and ¼ teaspoon pepper to the skillet and toss to combine.

ravioli with grape tomatoes and wine

hands-on time: 25 minutes / total time: 25 minutes
serves 4

16 to 18 ounces cheese ravioli (fresh or frozen)
 2 tablespoons olive oil
 2 shallots, chopped
 1 pint grape tomatoes, halved
 1 cup dry white wine
    Kosher salt and black pepper
 2 tablespoons unsalted butter
¼ cup chopped fresh flat-leaf parsley

▸ Cook the pasta according to the package directions.

▸ Meanwhile, heat the oil in a large skillet over medium heat. Add the shallots and cook, stirring occasionally, until soft, 3 to 5 minutes. Add the tomatoes, wine, ½ teaspoon salt, and ¼ teaspoon pepper and simmer until the tomatoes begin to soften, 4 to 5 minutes.

▸ Add the pasta, butter, and parsley to the skillet and toss to combine.

creamy ravioli and pesto gratin

hands-on time: 10 minutes / total time: 40 minutes
serves 4

16 to 18 ounces cheese ravioli (fresh or frozen)
 1 cup heavy cream
¼ cup pesto
¼ cup grated Parmesan (1 ounce)

▸ Heat oven to 400° F. Cook the pasta according to the package directions.

▸ In a large bowl, whisk together the cream and pesto. Add the pasta and toss to combine.

▸ Transfer the mixture to a shallow 2-quart baking dish and sprinkle with the Parmesan. Bake until golden brown and bubbling, 20 to 25 minutes.

fettuccine with lima beans, peas, and leeks

hands-on time: 25 minutes / total time: 25 minutes / serves 4

12 ounces fettuccine (³/₄ box)
 1 10-ounce package frozen
   lima beans (about 1¹/₂ cups)
 1 cup frozen peas
 2 tablespoons olive oil
 2 leeks (white and light green
   parts), halved lengthwise and
   sliced crosswise
   Kosher salt and black pepper
³/₄ cup heavy cream
 2 tablespoons chopped fresh
   tarragon
¹/₄ cup grated pecorino or
   Parmesan (1 ounce)

▶ Cook the pasta according to the package directions, adding the beans and peas during the last 2 minutes of cooking; drain.

▶ Meanwhile, heat the oil in a large skillet over medium heat. Add the leeks and season with ¹/₂ teaspoon salt and ¹/₄ teaspoon pepper. Cook, stirring occasionally, until tender (but not brown), 8 to 10 minutes. Add the cream and cook until slightly thickened, 3 to 4 minutes more.

▶ Add the pasta and tarragon to the skillet and toss to combine. Sprinkle with the pecorino before serving.

TIP
To clean leeks, fill a bowl with cold water, add the cut leeks, and swish them around a few times. With your hands loosely cupped, scoop up the leeks and place them on a plate. (The grit will be left behind in the bowl.) Discard the water and grit and repeat until the water remains clear.

rigatoni peperonata

hands-on time: 25 minutes / total time: 25 minutes / serves 4

¼ cup pine nuts

12 ounces rigatoni (¾ box)

¼ cup olive oil

3 bell peppers (preferably red and yellow), cut into ½-inch pieces

½ cup pitted kalamata olives, halved

¼ cup chopped fresh flat-leaf parsley

2 tablespoons chopped capers

2 tablespoons red wine vinegar

¼ teaspoon crushed red pepper
   Kosher salt and black pepper

▶ Heat oven to 400° F. Spread the pine nuts on a rimmed baking sheet and toast, tossing occasionally, until golden brown, 4 to 6 minutes. Cook the pasta according to the package directions.

▶ Meanwhile, heat the oil in a large skillet over medium-high heat. Add the bell peppers and cook, stirring occasionally, until tender, 5 to 6 minutes. Add the olives, parsley, capers, vinegar, crushed red pepper, and ¼ teaspoon each salt and black pepper and cook, stirring, until heated through, 1 to 2 minutes.

▶ Add the pasta and pine nuts to the skillet and cook, tossing, until heated through, 1 minute.

TIP
Peperonata, made with sautéed peppers and olive oil (and sometimes onions, garlic, and tomatoes), is a classic Mediterranean condiment. Cook a double batch and try it on crostini, layered in sandwiches, or as a topping for chicken, steak, or fish.

spaghetti with shrimp, Feta, and dill

hands-on time: 25 minutes / **total time: 25 minutes** / serves 4

12 ounces spaghetti (³⁄₄ box)
¼ cup plus 1 tablespoon
   olive oil
1 pound peeled and deveined
   large shrimp
   Kosher salt and black pepper
2 tablespoons fresh lemon juice
1 teaspoon grated lemon zest
3 ounces Feta, crumbled
   (³⁄₄ cup)
2 tablespoons coarsely chopped
   fresh dill

▶ Cook the pasta according to the package directions; drain and return it to the pot.

▶ Meanwhile, heat 1 tablespoon of the oil in a large skillet over medium-high heat. Season the shrimp with ½ teaspoon salt and ¼ teaspoon pepper and cook, tossing occasionally, until opaque throughout, 3 to 4 minutes. Stir in the lemon juice and zest.

▶ Add the shrimp mixture to the pasta, along with the Feta, dill, the remaining ¼ cup of oil, and ¼ teaspoon each salt and pepper. Toss to combine.

TIP
Crumbled Feta sold in supermarkets can be dry, flavorless, and treated with additives that prevent caking. It's worth buying a block of cheese and crumbling it yourself.

spinach and ricotta–stuffed shells

hands-on time: 20 minutes / **total time: 45 minutes** / **serves 4**

20 jumbo pasta shells (about
    half a 12-ounce box)
 1 24-ounce jar marinara sauce
 2 15-ounce containers ricotta
 2 cups baby spinach, chopped
½ cup grated Parmesan
    (2 ounces)
    Kosher salt and black pepper
 4 ounces mozzarella, grated
    (1 cup)
    Green salad (optional)

▶ Set an oven rack to the highest position and heat oven to 400° F. Cook the shells according to the package directions; drain and run under cold water to cool.

▶ Spread the marinara sauce in the bottom of a large broilerproof baking dish.

▶ In a bowl, combine the ricotta, spinach, Parmesan, ½ teaspoon salt, and ¼ teaspoon pepper. Spoon the mixture into the shells and place them on top of the sauce in the baking dish. Sprinkle with the mozzarella and bake until the shells are heated through, 10 to 12 minutes.

▶ Increase heat to broil. Broil the shells until the mozzarella begins to brown, 2 to 5 minutes. Serve with the salad, if desired.

TIP
Want to sneak an extra helping of green vegetables into this dish? Chop up cooked green beans, broccoli, or asparagus and fold it into the ricotta mixture along with the spinach.

dinner tonight:
vegetarian

potato, leek, and Feta tart

hands-on time: 20 minutes / total time: 1 hour, 20 minutes / serves 4

1 tablespoon olive oil

2 leeks (white and light green parts), halved lengthwise and sliced crosswise

2 small zucchini, halved lengthwise and sliced crosswise
Kosher salt and black pepper

2 ounces Feta, crumbled ($\frac{1}{2}$ cup)

2 tablespoons chopped fresh dill

$\frac{1}{2}$ pound small red potatoes (about 2)

1 piecrust (store-bought or homemade)

▶ Heat oven to 375° F. Heat the oil in a large skillet over medium heat. Add the leeks, zucchini, ½ teaspoon salt, and ¼ teaspoon pepper and cook, tossing occasionally, until just tender, 4 to 5 minutes. Fold in the Feta and dill. Add the potatoes and toss to combine.

▶ On a piece of parchment paper, roll the piecrust to a 12-inch diameter. Slide the paper (with the piecrust) onto a baking sheet. Spoon the potato mixture onto the piecrust, leaving a 2-inch border. Fold the border of the piecrust over the potato mixture. Bake until the piecrust is golden brown (cover the edges with foil if they start to get too dark) and the potatoes are tender, 50 to 60 minutes.

TIP
For a low-fat version of this dish, use pizza dough (regular or whole wheat). There's no need to fold over the sides, and the cooking time will be slightly shorter.

stir-fried rice noodles with tofu and vegetables

hands-on time: 25 minutes / total time: 25 minutes / serves 4

1 8-ounce package rice noodles or 12 ounces linguine
¼ cup brown sugar
¼ cup low-sodium soy sauce
2 tablespoons fresh lime juice
1 14-ounce package firm tofu, sliced ½ inch thick
1 tablespoon canola oil
2 carrots, cut into thin strips
1 red bell pepper, thinly sliced
1 tablespoon grated fresh ginger
2 cups bean sprouts
4 scallions, thinly sliced
¼ cup roasted peanuts, roughly chopped
½ cup fresh cilantro sprigs

▶ Cook the noodles according to the package directions. Drain and return them to the pot.

▶ Meanwhile, in a small bowl, whisk together the sugar, soy sauce, and lime juice. Gently press the tofu slices between layers of paper towels to remove excess liquid, then cut into ½-inch pieces.

▶ Heat the oil in a large skillet over medium-high heat. Add the carrots, bell pepper, and ginger and cook, tossing frequently, for 2 minutes. Add the tofu and bean sprouts and cook, tossing occasionally, until the vegetables are slightly tender, 3 to 4 minutes more.

▶ Add half the soy sauce mixture to the noodles and cook over medium-high heat, tossing occasionally, until heated through, 1 to 2 minutes.

▶ Transfer the noodles to a platter. Top with the carrot mixture, scallions, peanuts, cilantro, and the remaining soy sauce mixture.

TIP
Cilantro sprigs can be used (or chopped) whole—there's no need to remove the sweet, tender stems.

tofu tacos with spinach, corn, and goat cheese

hands-on time: 20 minutes / total time: 20 minutes / serves 4

1 tablespoon olive oil

1 14-ounce package extra-firm tofu—drained, patted dry, and crumbled

1½ teaspoons chili powder
    Kosher salt and black pepper

1 10-ounce package frozen corn (2 cups)

6 cups baby spinach (about 5 ounces)

8 small flour tortillas, warmed

3 ounces fresh goat cheese, crumbled (¾ cup)

¾ cup store-bought fresh salsa

▶ Heat the oil in a large nonstick skillet over medium-high heat. Add the tofu, chili powder, ½ teaspoon salt, and ¼ teaspoon pepper and cook, tossing occasionally, until golden brown, 4 to 5 minutes.

▶ Add the corn to the skillet and cook, tossing, until heated through, 2 to 3 minutes. Add the spinach and ½ teaspoon each salt and pepper and toss until the spinach is wilted, 1 to 2 minutes.

▶ Fill the tortillas with the tofu mixture, goat cheese, and salsa.

TIP
To warm the tortillas, wrap a stack of them in foil and heat in a 350° F oven for 8 to 10 minutes.

eggplant lasagna with fresh basil

hands-on time: 20 minutes / total time: 50 minutes / serves 4

½ pound plum tomatoes, halved and seeded
1 clove garlic
4 tablespoons olive oil
  Kosher salt and black pepper
2 eggplants (about 3 pounds), sliced lengthwise ¼ inch thick
1 cup ricotta
1 large egg
¼ cup chopped fresh basil
¼ cup grated Asiago or Parmesan (1 ounce)
4 cups mixed greens

▶ Heat broiler. In a food processor, puree the tomatoes and garlic with 1 tablespoon of the oil and ¼ teaspoon each salt and pepper.

▶ Arrange the eggplants on 2 broilerproof rimmed baking sheets, brush on both sides with 2 tablespoons of the remaining oil, and season with ½ teaspoon salt and ¼ teaspoon pepper. One sheet at a time, broil until charred and tender, 3 to 4 minutes per side.

▶ Meanwhile, in a small bowl, combine the ricotta, egg, basil, and ¼ teaspoon each salt and pepper.

▶ On the bottom of an 8-inch square baking dish, spread half the tomato sauce. Top with a third of the eggplant and half the ricotta mixture; repeat. Top with the remaining eggplant and tomato sauce and sprinkle with the Asiago.

▶ Reduce oven to 400° F. Bake the lasagna until bubbling, 15 to 20 minutes. Let rest for 10 minutes before serving.

▶ In a large bowl, toss the greens with the remaining tablespoon of oil and ¼ teaspoon each salt and pepper. Serve with the lasagna.

TIP
Eggplants are tastiest when less than 1½ pounds. And they should feel heavy for their size. Larger, older ones tend to be bitter.

skillet-poached huevos rancheros

hands-on time: 15 minutes / total time: 15 minutes / serves 4

1 16-ounce jar salsa (2 cups)
1 15.5-ounce can black beans, rinsed
4 large eggs
  Kosher salt and black pepper
2 scallions, sliced
¼ cup chopped fresh cilantro
4 small flour tortillas, warmed
½ cup sour cream

▶ In a large skillet, combine the salsa and beans and bring to a simmer.

▶ Make 4 small wells in the bean mixture. One at a time, crack each egg into a small bowl and slide it gently into a well. Season with ½ teaspoon salt and ¼ teaspoon pepper. Cook, covered, over medium heat, 3 to 5 minutes for slightly runny yolks.

▶ Sprinkle with the scallions and cilantro. Serve with the tortillas and sour cream.

TIP
Add the eggs to the pan just before serving or they'll quickly become overcooked.

dinner tonight:
desserts

caramel-almond ice cream torte

hands-on time: 15 minutes / total time: 1 hour, 20 minutes (includes freezing) / serves 12

½ cup sliced almonds
½ gallon (4 pints) vanilla ice
  cream, softened
1 cup caramel sauce (slightly
  warmed, if thick)

▶ Heat oven to 350° F. Spread the almonds on a rimmed baking sheet and toast, tossing occasionally, until golden, 4 to 6 minutes; let cool.

▶ Press the ice cream into a 9-inch springform pan. Freeze until slightly firm, 10 to 15 minutes.

▶ Top the ice cream with the caramel sauce and almonds and freeze until firm, at least 1 hour and up to 2 days. To serve, remove the torte from the pan and cut it into wedges.

TIP
No time to let your ice cream soften at room temperature? Microwave it in its cardboard container (top removed) on high in 10-second intervals until it reaches the desired consistency.

raspberry ice

hands-on time: 30 minutes / total time: 4$\frac{1}{2}$ hours (includes freezing) / serves 4

$\frac{1}{2}$ cup granulated sugar

3 cups raspberries, plus more for serving

$\frac{1}{2}$ cup heavy cream

▶ In a small saucepan, combine the sugar and 1 cup water. Bring to a boil, stirring to melt the sugar; let cool.

▶ In a blender, puree the raspberries with the sugar syrup. Strain into a loaf pan or shallow freezer-safe dish and freeze until firm, at least 4 hours and up to 1 day.

▶ When ready to serve, whip the cream until soft peaks form.

▶ Using a fork, scrape the surface of the frozen raspberry mixture to create icy flakes. Serve with the whipped cream and additional raspberries.

TIP
If fresh raspberries are not in season, you can use thawed frozen raspberries.

classic chocolate layer cake

hands-on time: 45 minutes / total time: 2 hours (includes cooling) / serves 8

For the cake

- 1 cup (2 sticks) unsalted butter, cut into pieces, plus more for the pans
- 2 cups all-purpose flour, spooned and leveled
- 1½ cups granulated sugar
- ½ cup packed dark brown sugar
- ¾ cup unsweetened cocoa powder
- 1 teaspoon baking soda
- 1 teaspoon kosher salt
- 2 large eggs
- ½ cup sour cream
- 1 teaspoon pure vanilla extract

For the frosting

- 24 ounces semisweet chocolate, chopped
- 1½ cups (3 sticks) unsalted butter, at room temperature

▶ Make the cake: Heat oven to 350° F. Butter two 8- or 9-inch round cake pans and line each with a round of parchment paper.

▶ In a large bowl, whisk together the flour, sugars, cocoa powder, baking soda, and salt.

▶ In a small saucepan, combine the butter and 1 cup water and bring to a boil. Add to the flour mixture and, using an electric mixer, mix on low speed until combined. Beat in the eggs, one at a time, then the sour cream and vanilla.

▶ Transfer the batter to the prepared pans. Bake until a toothpick inserted in the center comes out clean, 35 to 45 minutes. Let cool in the pans for 20 minutes, then turn out onto racks to cool completely.

▶ Meanwhile, make the frosting: In a heatproof bowl set over (not in) a saucepan of simmering water, melt the chocolate, stirring often, until smooth. Let cool to room temperature (do not let solidify).

▶ Using an electric mixer, beat the butter on medium-high speed until fluffy, 1 to 2 minutes. Slowly add the chocolate and beat until smooth.

▶ Transfer one of the cooled cakes to a platter and spread with ¾ cup of the frosting. Top with the remaining cake and spread with the remaining frosting.

TIP

For flat, easy-to-layer cake rounds, turn them out of the pans onto cooling racks bottom-sides up. The domed tops will flatten as the cakes cool.

poached-apricot sundaes with coconut

hands-on time: 15 minutes / total time: 35 minutes
serves 4

- ¼ cup sweetened shredded coconut
- ½ cup honey
- 2 strips lemon zest, removed with a vegetable peeler
- 4 apricots, quartered
- 1 pint vanilla ice cream

▶ Heat oven to 350° F. Spread the coconut on a rimmed baking sheet and bake, tossing occasionally, until golden, 4 to 6 minutes.

▶ In a small saucepan, combine the honey, lemon zest, and 1 cup water; bring to a boil. Add the apricots and transfer to a medium bowl. Refrigerate until cool.

▶ Divide the ice cream and apricots among bowls and top with the honey syrup (discarding the zest) and coconut.

banana-rum sundaes with toasted pecans

hands-on time: 15 minutes / total time: 15 minutes
serves 4

- ¼ cup pecans
- ½ cup heavy cream
- 1 tablespoon granulated sugar
- 1 pint vanilla ice cream
- 2 bananas, sliced
- ¼ cup dark rum

▶ Heat oven to 350° F. Spread the pecans on a rimmed baking sheet and bake, tossing occasionally, until fragrant, 6 to 8 minutes. Let cool, then roughly chop.

▶ In a large bowl, beat the cream with the sugar until soft peaks form.

▶ Divide the ice cream among bowls and top with the bananas, whipped cream, rum, and pecans.

gin-spiked blueberry sundaes

hands-on time: 10 minutes / total time: 30 minutes
serves 4

  1 cup blueberries
 ⅓ cup gin
  1 pint vanilla ice cream

▶ In a small saucepan, combine the blueberries and gin. Simmer, stirring frequently, until the berries burst and the mixture begins to thicken, 5 to 8 minutes. Transfer to a small bowl. Refrigerate until cool.

▶ Divide the ice cream among bowls and top with the blueberry sauce.

cinnamon-crisp sundaes with chocolate sauce

hands-on time: 10 minutes / total time: 10 minutes
serves 4

  3 tablespoons unsalted butter
  2 tablespoons granulated sugar
  4 6-inch flour tortillas, cut into thin strips
 ½ teaspoon ground cinnamon
  1 pint vanilla ice cream
 ½ cup chocolate sauce

▶ In a large skillet, melt the butter and sugar over medium heat. Add the tortillas and cook, tossing, until crisp, 3 to 5 minutes. Transfer to a plate and sprinkle with the cinnamon.

▶ Divide the ice cream among bowls and top with the chocolate sauce and cinnamon crisps.

peanut butter cup cookies

hands-on time: 15 minutes / total time: 40 minutes / makes 48 cookies

1½ cups all-purpose flour,
   spooned and leveled
 1 teaspoon baking soda
½ teaspoon kosher salt
½ cup (1 stick) unsalted butter,
   at room temperature
¾ cup packed dark brown sugar
½ cup granulated sugar
 1 large egg
 1 teaspoon pure vanilla extract
 1 12-ounce package miniature
   peanut butter cups, coarsely
   chopped

▶ Heat oven to 375° F. In a medium bowl, whisk together the flour, baking soda, and salt.

▶ Using an electric mixer, beat the butter and sugars on medium-high until fluffy, 2 to 3 minutes. Add the egg and vanilla and beat to combine. Reduce speed to low and gradually add the flour mixture, mixing until just combined (do not overmix). Fold in the peanut butter cups by hand.

▶ Drop tablespoonfuls of the dough onto 2 parchment-lined baking sheets, spacing them 2 inches apart. Bake until the cookies are light brown around the edges, 12 to 15 minutes. Cool slightly on the baking sheets, then transfer to wire racks to cool completely.

TIP
The cookies can be stored at room temperature in an airtight container for up to 3 days.

chocolate-ricotta icebox cake

hands-on time: 15 minutes / **total time: 12 hours, 15 minutes (includes chilling)** / **serves 8**

Nonstick cooking spray

2 15-ounce containers ricotta

12 ounces semisweet chocolate, melted and cooled, plus more, shaved, for topping

½ 9-ounce package chocolate wafer cookies

▶ Spray an 8½-by-4½-inch loaf pan with the cooking spray. Line the pan with 2 crisscrossed pieces of parchment paper, spraying between the layers (to keep them in place) and leaving an overhang on each side.

▶ In a food processor, puree the ricotta with the melted chocolate until very smooth, about 1 minute.

▶ Layer a third of the ricotta mixture, then half the cookies, in the pan; repeat, then top with the remaining ricotta mixture. Refrigerate for at least 12 hours and up to 2 days.

▶ Using the parchment overhang, lift the cake out of the pan, transfer to a platter, and slice. Sprinkle with the shaved chocolate.

TIP

For a silky-smooth filling, make sure you process the ricotta and chocolate long enough and occasionally scrape down the side of the food-processor bowl.

A by-the-numbers guide to
what's in every recipe.

RECIPE KEY

 30 MINUTES OR LESS

♥ HEART-HEALTHY

🍲 ONE-POT MEAL

🌱 VEGETARIAN

✖ NO-COOK

🔆 FAMILY-FRIENDLY

APPETIZERS

8 prosciutto-fennel crostini

PER 3-PIECE SERVING: 198 calories; 9g fat
(2g sat. fat); 22mg chol.; 1,020mg sodium;
12g protein; 20g carbs; 1g sugar; 2g fiber;
2mg iron; 30mg calcium.

8 radishes with creamy ricotta

PER SERVING: 141 calories; 11g fat (6g sat. fat);
32mg chol.; 119mg sodium; 7g protein; 3g carbs;
1g sugar; 0g fiber; 0mg iron; 133mg calcium.

9 smoked salmon pizzettes

PER PIZZETTE: 512 calories; 18g fat (6g sat. fat);
60mg chol.; 772mg sodium; 28g protein; 63g
carbs; 4g sugar; 2g fiber; 4mg iron; 33mg calcium.

9 grilled teriyaki wings

PER 2-PIECE SERVING: 214 calories; 13g fat (4g sat.
fat); 57mg chol.; 667mg sodium; 19g protein;
2g carbs; 2g sugar; 0g fiber; 1mg iron; 11mg
calcium.

11 artichoke and spinach relish with walnuts

PER 3-TABLESPOON SERVING: 91 calories; 7g fat
(1g sat. fat); 4mg chol.; 274mg sodium;
3g protein; 4g carbs; 0g sugar; 2g fiber; 0mg
iron; 56mg calcium.

11 creamy salmon spread with horseradish

PER 3-TABLESPOON SERVING: 154 calories; 12g fat
(6g sat. fat); 50mg chol.; 364mg sodium;
10g protein; 3g carbs; 2g sugar; 0g fiber; 0mg
iron; 13mg calcium.

12 double tomato crostini

PER 3-PIECE SERVING: 156 calories; 3g fat (0g sat.
fat); 1mg chol.; 468mg sodium; 6g protein; 27g
carbs; 2g sugar; 3g fiber; 2mg iron; 33mg calcium.

12 five-minute hummus

PER ¼-CUP SERVING: 187 calories; 13g fat (2g sat.
fat); 0mg chol.; 428mg sodium; 5g protein; 14g
carbs; 1g sugar; 4g fiber; 1mg iron; 35mg calcium.

13 shrimp skewers with Feta-dill sauce

PER 2-PIECE SERVING: 308 calories; 22g fat (5g sat.
fat); 185mg chol.; 447mg sodium; 25g protein;
2g carbs; 1g sugar; 0g fiber; 3mg iron; 130mg
calcium.

13 sweet pea and ricotta crostini

PER 4-PIECE SERVING: 424 calories; 21g fat (6g sat.
fat); 21mg chol.; 841mg sodium; 17g protein;
43g carbs; 5g sugar; 5g fiber; 3mg iron; 209mg
calcium.

SALADS

17 creamy shrimp salad with endive and cucumber

PER SERVING: 216 calories; 5g fat (2g sat. fat);
183mg chol.; 483mg sodium; 28g protein;
14g carbs; 3g sugar; 9g fiber; 5mg iron; 247mg
calcium.

19 turkey Waldorf salad

PER SERVING: 186 calories; 11g fat (2g sat. fat);
32mg chol.; 330mg sodium; 13g protein;
10g carbs; 6g sugar; 2g fiber; 2mg iron; 48mg
calcium.

21 minty bulgur salad with salmon and cucumbers

PER SERVING: 380 calories; 14g fat (2g sat. fat);
72mg chol.; 436mg sodium; 32g protein; 35g
carbs; 3g sugar; 8g fiber; 4mg iron; 87mg calcium.

22 romaine salad with tomatoes and bacon

PER SERVING: 153 calories; 13g fat (3g sat. fat);
12mg chol.; 251mg sodium; 6g protein; 6g carbs;
3g sugar; 3g fiber; 1mg iron; 106mg calcium.

22 mesclun salad with chickpeas and dried cherries
PER SERVING: 247 calories; 11g fat (1g sat. fat); 0mg chol.; 326mg sodium; 6g protein; 32g carbs; 14g sugar; 7g fiber; 2mg iron; 47mg calcium.

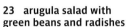

23 arugula salad with green beans and radishes
PER SERVING: 134 calories; 10g fat (2g sat. fat); 6mg chol.; 156mg sodium; 4g protein; 8g carbs; 1g sugar; 3g fiber; 1mg iron; 152mg calcium.

23 watercress salad with beets and Feta
PER SERVING: 146 calories; 10g fat (3g sat. fat); 13mg chol.; 506mg sodium; 4g protein; 12g carbs; 8g sugar; 2g fiber; 2mg iron; 148mg calcium.

25 chopped steak salad
PER SERVING: 252 calories; 10g fat (3g sat. fat); 30mg chol.; 731mg sodium; 23g protein; 18g carbs; 5g sugar; 4g fiber; 3mg iron; 86mg calcium.

27 Moroccan chicken salad with carrots
PER SERVING: 433 calories; 21g fat (3g sat. fat); 94mg chol.; 667mg sodium; 37g protein; 26g carbs; 14g sugar; 5g fiber; 3mg iron; 83mg calcium.

29 grilled salmon salad with grapefruit
PER SERVING: 441 calories; 26g fat (4g sat. fat); 108mg chol.; 469mg sodium; 41g protein; 12g carbs; 6g sugar; 5g fiber; 2mg iron; 38mg calcium.

POULTRY

33 braised chicken and spring vegetables
PER SERVING: 273 calories; 13g fat (3.5g sat. fat); 100mg chol.; 426mg sodium; 29g protein; 9g carbs; 5g sugar; 2g fiber; 2mg iron; 47mg calcium.

35 Havarti-stuffed chicken breasts with tomato salad
PER SERVING: 334 calories; 18g fat (9g sat. fat); 119mg chol.; 474mg sodium; 39g protein; 0g carbs; 0g sugar; 0g fiber; 1mg iron; 220mg calcium.

37 spiced chicken with couscous salad
PER SERVING: 433 calories; 15g fat (3g sat. fat); 94mg chol.; 575mg sodium; 41g protein; 34g carbs; 4g sugar; 4g fiber; 3mg iron; 71mg calcium.

39 spicy orange-glazed drumsticks with green beans
PER SERVING: 542 calories; 16g fat (5g sat. fat); 102mg chol.; 974mg sodium; 37g protein; 64g carbs; 19g sugar; 7g fiber; 4mg iron; 314mg calcium.

41 chicken and prosciutto club sandwiches
PER SERVING: 472 calories; 27g fat (5g sat. fat); 76mg chol.; 1,434mg sodium; 30g protein; 26g carbs; 3g sugar; 1g fiber; 3mg iron; 93mg calcium.

43 roasted chicken with carrots and potatoes
PER SERVING: 598 calories; 31g fat (10g sat. fat); 134mg chol.; 672mg sodium; 41g protein; 38g carbs; 7g sugar; 6g fiber; 4mg iron; 81mg calcium.

45 crispy turkey cutlets with green bean salad
PER SERVING: 448 calories; 22g fat (3g sat. fat); 151mg chol.; 873mg sodium; 37g protein; 28g carbs; 3g sugar; 4g fiber; 4mg iron; 79mg calcium.

47 chicken and chorizo tostadas
PER SERVING: 608 calories; 40g fat (19g sat. fat); 141mg chol.; 1,191mg sodium; 41g protein; 18g carbs; 1g sugar; 1g fiber; 3mg iron; 470mg calcium.

49 chicken with spinach and mushrooms
PER SERVING: 295 calories; 11g fat (2g sat. fat); 94mg chol.; 615mg sodium; 38g protein; 7g carbs; 3g sugar; 2g fiber; 3mg iron; 84mg calcium.

51 Thai red curry chicken
PER SERVING: 700 calories; 38g fat (22g sat. fat); 94mg chol.; 519mg sodium; 41g protein; 49g carbs; 2g sugar; 4g fiber; 7mg iron; 66mg calcium.

55 grilled beef and pepper fajitas
PER SERVING: 547 calories; 28g fat (9g sat. fat); 60mg chol.; 834mg sodium; 32g protein; 42g carbs; 5g sugar; 6g fiber; 4mg iron; 135mg calcium.

57 Gouda cheeseburgers with fennel-onion relish
PER SERVING: 876 calories; 43g fat (15g sat. fat); 160mg chol.; 1,424mg sodium; 55g protein; 67g carbs; 16g sugar; 9g fiber; 7mg iron; 354mg calcium.

59 grilled steak, plums, and bok choy
PER SERVING: 335 calories; 15g fat (5g sat. fat); 60mg chol.; 1,327mg sodium; 39g protein; 10g carbs; 9g sugar; 2g fiber; 3mg iron; 38mg calcium.

61 lamb chops with curried rice and cherries
PER SERVING: 415 calories; 10g fat (3g sat. fat); 87mg chol.; 318mg sodium; 31g protein; 52g carbs; 5g sugar; 3g fiber; 4mg iron; 34mg calcium.

63 steak with potato salad and blue cheese vinaigrette
PER SERVING: 390 calories; 14g fat (6g sat. fat); 79mg chol.; 898mg sodium; 43g protein; 21g carbs; 1g sugar; 3g fiber; 5mg iron; 83mg calcium.

65 slow-cooker corned beef, Brussels sprouts, and carrots
PER SERVING: 512 calories; 31g fat (12g sat. fat); 152mg chol.; 1,729mg sodium; 30g protein; 22g carbs; 8g sugar; 6g fiber; 4mg iron; 99mg calcium.

67 deep-dish cheeseburger pizza
PER SERVING: 606 calories; 28g fat (10g sat. fat); 64mg chol.; 788mg sodium; 29g protein; 64g carbs; 8g sugar; 3g fiber; 5mg iron; 223mg calcium.

69 spicy beef kebabs with minted watermelon salad
PER SERVING: 361 calories; 14g fat (5g sat. fat); 111mg chol.; 458mg sodium; 38g protein; 24g carbs; 19g sugar; 2g fiber; 5mg iron; 45mg calcium.

71 lamb with golden Israeli couscous

PER SERVING: 650 calories; 32g fat (11g sat. fat); 131mg chol.; 868mg sodium; 40g protein; 50g carbs; 11g sugar; 5g fiber; 6mg iron; 62mg calcium.

73 sweet and spicy beef stir-fry

PER SERVING: 462 calories; 11g fat (3g sat. fat); 40mg chol.; 638mg sodium; 33g protein; 59g carbs; 23g sugar; 4g fiber; 5mg iron; 66mg calcium.

PORK

77 roasted pork chops and peaches

PER SERVING: 532 calories; 14g fat (4g sat. fat); 92mg chol.; 435mg sodium; 44g protein; 59g carbs; 6g sugar; 4g fiber; 3mg iron; 72mg calcium.

79 meatballs with pine nuts and raisins

PER SERVING: 509 calories; 39g fat (12g sat. fat); 102mg chol.; 1,169mg sodium; 29g protein; 11g carbs; 3g sugar; 5g fiber; 7mg iron; 149mg calcium.

81 tapas plate with marinated chickpeas

PER SERVING: 706 calories; 38g fat (17g sat. fat); 82mg chol.; 2,083mg sodium; 33g protein; 59g carbs; 17g sugar; 8g fiber; 4mg iron; 717mg calcium.

83 gingery pork and cucumber pitas

PER SERVING: 516 calories; 23g fat (7g sat. fat); 80mg chol.; 766mg sodium; 29g protein; 49g carbs; 10g sugar; 3g fiber; 3mg iron; 100mg calcium.

85 pork chops with garlicky broccoli

PER SERVING: 474 calories; 17g fat (4g sat. fat); 61mg chol.; 506mg sodium; 30g protein; 50g carbs; 1g sugar; 3g fiber; 3mg iron; 97mg calcium.

87 apricot-glazed ham with potatoes and asparagus

PER SERVING: 443 calories; 19g fat (4g sat. fat); 109mg chol.; 2,042mg sodium; 41g protein; 28g carbs; 9g sugar; 3g fiber; 4mg iron; 37mg calcium.

89 ham, Gruyère, and shallot pizza

PER SERVING: 305 calories; 10g fat (3g sat. fat); 24mg chol.; 865mg sodium; 16g protein; 38g carbs; 3g sugar; 2g fiber; 3mg iron; 111mg calcium.

91 paprika-spiced pork chops with spinach sauté

PER SERVING: 345 calories; 16g fat (5g sat. fat); 91mg chol.; 472mg sodium; 39g protein; 12g carbs; 6g sugar; 3g fiber; 4mg iron; 116mg calcium.

93 brown sugar–glazed pork with grilled corn

PER SERVING: 342 calories; 12g fat (5g sat. fat); 108mg chol.; 670mg sodium; 33g protein; 28g carbs; 12g sugar; 3g fiber; 3mg iron; 42mg calcium.

SEAFOOD

97 salmon with brown butter, almonds, and green beans

PER SERVING: 396 calories; 25g fat (9g sat. fat); 120mg chol.; 506mg sodium; 36g protein; 9g carbs; 2g sugar; 4g fiber; 3mg iron; 77mg calcium.

99 mussels with pesto and garlic oven fries

PER SERVING: 631 calories; 26g fat (6g sat. fat); 74mg chol.; 1,261mg sodium; 38g protein; 54g carbs; 2g sugar; 4g fiber; 12mg iron; 319mg calcium.

101 ancho-rubbed salmon with summer squash

PER SERVING: 315 calories; 17g fat (3g sat. fat); 90mg chol.; 564mg sodium; 33g protein; 6g carbs; 5g sugar; 1g fiber; 2mg iron; 37mg calcium.

103 curried shrimp rolls

PER SERVING: 312 calories; 14g fat (2g sat. fat); 173mg chol.; 612mg sodium; 22g protein; 23g carbs; 3g sugar; 1g fiber; 4mg iron; 112mg calcium.

105 seared scallops with snow peas and orange

PER SERVING: 343 calories; 7g fat (1g sat. fat); 43mg chol.; 455mg sodium; 27g protein; 45g carbs; 4g sugar; 4g fiber; 4mg iron; 78mg calcium.

107 shrimp and bacon with Cheddar grits

PER SERVING: 447 calories; 17g fat (8g sat. fat); 211mg chol.; 1,067mg sodium; 36g protein; 36g carbs; 1g sugar; 1g fiber; 5mg iron; 280mg calcium.

109 salmon kebabs with cilantro sauce

PER SERVING: 479 calories; 28g fat (4g sat. fat); 90mg chol.; 437mg sodium; 37g protein; 20g carbs; 3g sugar; 1g fiber; 3mg iron; 42mg calcium.

111 ginger-glazed cod with sautéed summer squash

PER SERVING: 253 calories; 10g fat (1g sat. fat); 65mg chol.; 556mg sodium; 29g protein; 13g carbs; 10g sugar; 2g fiber; 1mg iron; 52mg calcium.

PASTA

115 spaghetti with zucchini, walnuts, and raisins

PER SERVING: 641 calories; 23g fat (4g sat. fat); 5mg chol.; 387mg sodium; 20g protein; 94g carbs; 20g sugar; 8g fiber; 4mg iron; 171mg calcium.

117 pasta with chicken sausage and broccoli

PER SERVING: 512 calories; 11g fat (3g sat. fat); 40mg chol.; 431mg sodium; 27g protein; 80g carbs; 7g sugar; 8g fiber; 5mg iron; 204mg calcium.

118 ravioli with peas and crispy bacon

PER SERVING: 590 calories; 29g fat (13g sat. fat); 91mg chol.; 1,127mg sodium; 23g protein; 59g carbs; 6g sugar; 7g fiber; 3mg iron; 197mg calcium.

118   ravioli with brown butter and sage
PER SERVING: 568 calories; 34g fat (18g sat. fat); 110mg chol.; 837mg sodium; 17g protein; 50g carbs; 4g sugar; 4g fiber; 2mg iron; 185mg calcium.

119   ravioli with grape tomatoes and wine
PER SERVING: 510 calories; 23g fat (11g sat. fat); 80mg chol.; 842mg sodium; 16g protein; 55g carbs; 6g sugar; 4g fiber; 3mg iron; 179mg calcium.

119   creamy ravioli and pesto gratin
PER SERVING: 669 calories; 42g fat (23g sat. fat); 156mg chol.; 861mg sodium; 22g protein; 51g carbs; 3g sugar; 4g fiber; 2mg iron; 411mg calcium.

121   fettuccine with lima beans, peas, and leeks
PER SERVING: 684 calories; 27g fat (13g sat. fat); 66mg chol.; 317mg sodium; 22g protein; 90g carbs; 8g sugar; 9g fiber; 6mg iron; 202mg calcium.

123   rigatoni peperonata
PER SERVING: 563 calories; 25g fat (3g sat. fat); 0mg chol.; 523mg sodium; 13g protein; 74g carbs; 7g sugar; 4g fiber; 3mg iron; 23mg calcium.

125   spaghetti with shrimp, Feta, and dill
PER SERVING: 675 calories; 27g fat (7g sat. fat); 197mg chol.; 844mg sodium; 39g protein; 67g carbs; 3g sugar; 4g fiber; 6mg iron; 215mg calcium.

127   spinach and ricotta–stuffed shells
PER SERVING: 794 calories; 47g fat (24g sat. fat); 141mg chol.; 1,390mg sodium; 44g protein; 49g carbs; 9g sugar; 5g fiber; 3mg iron; 798mg calcium.

VEGETARIAN

131   potato, leek, and Feta tart
PER SERVING: 396 calories; 22g fat (9g sat. fat); 27mg chol.; 668mg sodium; 7g protein; 44g carbs; 6g sugar; 2g fiber; 2mg iron; 134mg calcium.

133   stir-fried rice noodles with tofu and vegetables
PER SERVING: 512 calories; 15g fat (1g sat. fat); 0mg chol.; 529mg sodium; 19g protein; 76g carbs; 17g sugar; 5g fiber; 4mg iron; 203mg calcium.

135   tofu tacos with spinach, corn, and goat cheese
PER SERVING: 355 calories; 14g fat (3g sat. fat); 7mg chol.; 646mg sodium; 18g protein; 46g carbs; 4g sugar; 7g fiber; 4mg iron; 289mg calcium.

137   eggplant lasagna with fresh basil
PER SERVING: 378 calories; 26g fat (9g sat. fat); 91mg chol.; 782mg sodium; 15g protein; 27g carbs; 11g sugar; 14g fiber; 2mg iron; 245mg calcium.

139   skillet-poached huevos rancheros
PER SERVING: 325 calories; 13g fat (6g sat. fat); 232mg chol.; 1,119mg sodium; 14g protein; 37g carbs; 7g sugar; 5g fiber; 3mg iron; 115mg calcium.

DESSERTS

143   caramel-almond ice cream torte
PER SERVING: 290 calories; 14g fat (7g sat. fat); 33mg chol.; 120mg sodium; 6g protein; 38g carbs; 32g sugar; 1g fiber; 0mg iron; 117mg calcium.

145   raspberry ice
PER SERVING: 193 calories; 6g fat (4g sat. fat); 21mg chol.; 7mg sodium; 1g protein; 36g carbs; 29g sugar; 6g fiber; 1mg iron; 31mg calcium.

147   classic chocolate layer cake
PER SERVING: 1,306 calories; 86g fat (54g sat. fat); 213mg chol.; 435mg sodium; 14g protein; 135g carbs; 100g sugar; 4g fiber; 5mg iron; 61mg calcium.

148   poached-apricot sundaes with coconut
PER SERVING: 328 calories; 11g fat (7g sat. fat); 25mg chol.; 52mg sodium; 3g protein; 56g carbs; 51g sugar; 1g fiber; 0mg iron; 90mg calcium.

148   banana-rum sundaes with toasted pecans
PER SERVING: 397 calories; 25g fat (12g sat. fat); 66mg chol.; 48mg sodium; 5g protein; 34g carbs; 25g sugar; 2g fiber; 0mg iron; 110mg calcium.

149   gin-spiked blueberry sundaes
PER SERVING: 188 calories; 9g fat (5g sat. fat); 25mg chol.; 35mg sodium; 3g protein; 20g carbs; 18g sugar; 1g fiber; 0mg iron; 82mg calcium.

149   cinnamon-crisp sundaes with chocolate sauce
PER SERVING: 450 calories; 20g fat (11g sat. fat); 48mg chol.; 265mg sodium; 7g protein; 62g carbs; 41g sugar; 1g fiber; 2mg iron; 127mg calcium.

151   peanut butter cup cookies
PER COOKIE: 90 calories; 4g fat (2g sat. fat); 10mg chol.; 72mg sodium; 1g protein; 12g carbs; 9g sugar; 0g fiber; 0mg iron; 10mg calcium.

153   chocolate-ricotta icebox cake
PER SERVING: 467 calories; 28g fat (17g sat. fat); 55mg chol.; 182mg sodium; 16g protein; 42g carbs; 29g sugar; 1g fiber; 2mg iron; 225mg calcium.

DINNER TONIGHT : **RECIPE INDEX**

REAL SIMPLE
managing editor Kristin van Ogtrop
creative director Janet Froelich
executive editor Sarah Humphreys
deputy managing editor Jacklyn Monk
managing editor, RealSimple.com
Kathleen Murray Harris

STAFF FOR THIS BOOK
food director Allie Lewis Clapp
art director Eva Spring
senior editor Lygeia Grace
food assistant Lindsay Funston
contributing editor Candy Gianetti
photo director Casey Tierney
deputy photo editor
Lauren Reichbach Epstein
photo archivist Brian Madigan
copy chief Nancy Negovetich
copy editors Benjamin Ake, Jenny Brown,
Pamela Grossman
research chief Westry Green
researcher Kaitlyn Pirie
art assistant Jennica Johnstone
production director Jeff Nesmith
production manager Joan Weinstein
imaging director Richard Prue
imaging manager Claudio Muller

publisher Kevin White
associate publisher Melissa Gasper
senior vice president, consumer marketing
Carrie Goldin
vice president, marketing Sarah Kate Ellis

TIME HOME ENTERTAINMENT
publisher Richard Fraiman
general manager Steven Sandonato
executive director, marketing services
Carol Pittard
director, retail & special sales Tom Mifsud
director, new product development
Peter Harper
director, bookazine development &
marketing Laura Adam

publishing director, brand marketing
Joy Butts
assistant general counsel Helen Wan
marketing manager Victoria Alfonso
design & prepress manager
Anne-Michelle Gallero
book production manager
Susan Chodakiewicz

SPECIAL THANKS
recipe developers Kristen Evans,
Cyd McDowell, Kate Merker, Sara
Quessenberry, Jenny Rosenstrach
recipe testers Kristen Evans, Vanessa
Seder, Susan Streight, Amy Vuoso,
Caroline Wright, Chelsea Zimmer
food stylists Victoria Granof, Jee Levin,
Cyd McDowell, Carrie Purcell,
Sara Quessenberry, Maggie Ruggiero,
Susan Spungen, Susan Sugarman,
Susie Theodorou
prop stylists Angharad Bailey, Jocelyne
Beaudoin, Heather Chontos, Helen
Crowther, Cindy DiPrima, Michele Faro,
Lynsey Fryers, Terry Mainord, PJ Mehaffey,
Jeffrey W. Miller, Pam Morris, Leslie
Siegel, Loren Simons, Theo Vamvounakis,
Deborah Williams, David Yarritu
thanks also to Christine Austin, Jeremy
Biloon, Glenn Buonocore, Jim Childs,
Rose Cirrincione, Jacqueline Fitzgerald,
Carrie Frazier, Lauren Hall, Kelly
Holechek, Suzanne Janso, Malena Jones,
Brynn Joyce, Mona Li, Robert Marasco,
Kimberly Marshall, Amy Migliaccio,
Brooke Reger, Dave Rozzelle, Ilene
Schreider, Adriana Tierno, Vanessa Wu

PHOTO CREDITS
COVER: Christopher Baker, photographer; Maggie Ruggiero, food stylist;
Jeffrey W. Miller, prop stylist

Quentin Bacon: *pages 64, 90, 104, 138*
Christopher Baker: *pages 8 (right), 9 (right),
12 (left), 34, 68, 92, 98, 130, 132, 136, 144,
149 (left), 152*

Ditte Isager: *page 12 (right)*
John Kernick: *page 150*
Yunhee Kim: *page 88*
Charles Masters: *pages 24, 54, 58, 72*
Ellie Miller: *pages 26, 40, 46, 50*
Marcus Nilsson: *pages 20, 32, 36, 80, 82,
86, 110, 116, 126*
José Picayo: *pages 13 (right), 38, 48, 78, 84*
Con Poulos: *pages 8 (left), 10, 22 (left,
right), 23 (left, right), 62, 76, 96, 120, 122,
134, 146*
David Prince: *pages 9 (left), 18, 66, 102,
106, 118 (left, right), 119 (left, right), 124,
142, 148 (left, right), 149 (right)*
Anna Williams: *page 42*
James Wojcik: *page 13 (left)*
Romulo Yanes: *pages 16, 28, 44, 56, 60, 70,
100, 108, 114*

Copyright © 2011
Time Home Entertainment Inc.
Published by Real Simple Books, an imprint of
Time Home Entertainment Inc.
135 West 50th Street
New York, NY 10020

First printing 2011
Printed in the USA

We welcome your comments and
suggestions about Real Simple Books. Please
e-mail us at books@realsimple.com.

To order any of our Collector's Edition books,
please call us at 1-800-327-6388 (Monday
through Friday, 7 A.M. to 8 P.M. CST, or
Saturday, 7 A.M. to 6 P.M. CST).